# THE PROGRAMME OF MODERNISM

# THE PROGRAMME OF MODERNISM

## A REPLY

TO THE ENCYCLICAL OF PIUS X., *Pascendi Dominici Gregis*

WITH THE TEXT OF THE ENCYCLICAL IN AN ENGLISH VERSION

TRANSLATED FROM THE ITALIAN

BY

REV. FATHER GEORGE TYRRELL

WITH AN INTRODUCTION

BY

A. LESLIE LILLEY

VICAR OF ST. MARY'S, PADDINGTON GREEN, LONDON

"That that dieth, let it die; and that that is to be cut off, let it be cut off."—*Zechariah*, xi, 9.

"Enlarge the place of thy tent, and let them stretch forth the curtains of thine habitations; spare not: lengthen thy cords, strengthen thy stakes. For thou shalt spread abroad on the right hand and on the left; and thy seed shall possess the nations, and make the desolate cities to be inhabited."—*Isaiah*, liv, 2-3.

WIPF & STOCK · Eugene, Oregon

Wipf and Stock Publishers
199 W 8th Ave, Suite 3
Eugene, OR 97401

The Programme of Modernism
A Reply to the Encyclical of Pius X, Pascendi Dominici Gregis,
with the Text of the Encyclical in an English Translation
By Tyrrell, George, SJ and Lilley, A. Leslie
ISBN 13: 678-1-62032-865-1
Publication date 1/15/2013
Previously published by G. P. Putnam's Sons, 1908

# INTRODUCTION

THOUGH written for Roman Catholics by Roman Catholics, the message of the following pages concerns a far wider world than that of even the largest Christian communion. Obviously it concerns every Christian body, without distinction, for they are all in some measure pressed by those problems which have now become so acute in the Roman Church—problems whose roots are in an age prior to the Protestant Reformation, prior to the schism of East and West, and whose fibres run up through all the diverging branches into which Christendom has been divided. Nay, more, those very divisions are, to a large extent, the result of a failure to appreciate the problems in question, and of a superficial estimate of the radical principles at issue. Such failure was perhaps inevitable before the accumulating evidence of historical and biblical criticism had lit up the darkness of the past with a brilliancy previously unattainable. In that light, the controversies that divide Christians seem trivial beside that in which they are forcibly united to-day for the defence of their common presuppositions. It seems more and more likely every day that this great controversy of faith with unfaith may drive them to seek refuge on a higher and firmer ground, where doctrinal and institutional differences will diminish if not vanish altogether. If such a ground is to some extent sketched out in this *Programme of Modernism*, it is not because that programme is less deeply and distinctively Catholic than that of Mediævalism, but because it is more so. And similarly, in the measure that other denominations "look unto the rock whence they were hewn"; in the measure that they search back to the root of their doctrinal and institutional life, namely, to those experiences of faith—of the Fatherhood of God, the atoning power of Christ, the consolation of the indwelling spirit—of which outward religion is but the instrument and expression, they will cease, not to value, but to over-value those differences of form and formula which may continue to separate them from the ancient and world-wide Catholic tradition. Heretofore re-union has been sought through the very principle of division—through a forced and artificial agreement on questions, not of faith, but of theology or observance viewed as of primary and essential importance. And such unity, bearing the seed of division in its heart, has always been short-lived. "Except the Lord build the house their labour is but lost that build it." No council, however universally representative, could effect more than a temporary and unstable compromise. No stable unity can be effected but by the slow self-revelation of irresistible Truth, whose forward march, like that of a glacier, none can withstand. "Whosoever shall fall upon that stone shall be broken, but on whomsoever it shall fall it will grind him to powder." This unity, which the pressure of accumulating evidence is forcing upon Christians, is not so much sought as found. A fog has lifted, and we who deemed ourselves far asunder find ourselves close together.

But the problems handled in this *Programme* affect not only Christianity, but religion in general. God wills, and wills effectively, that all men should be saved and should come to a knowledge of such truth as is needed for their salvation. When men knew but a corner of the world, and but a page or two of its voluminous history, it was possible to believe that God willed all men to be formally Christians, and not merely Christians in spirit. That is no longer possible. A knowledge and comparison of the countless religions of the present and of the past, a recognition of the psychological incapacity of all but a fraction of humanity to apprehend the theological conceptions of one particular race and epoch, force us, under pain of scepticism and pessimism, to acknowledge in every religion an effort of the all pervading Word to reveal the Father in forms and symbols suited to the mental and moral conditions of its votaries. It is Christ who has taught us that if salvation is pre-eminently of the Jews it is also in due measure of the Samaritans and the Gentiles. And the same note has been struck even more clearly by S. Paul, S. Justin, S. Clement of Alexandria, S. Augustine. To feel this relation of fraternity between the various members of the religious family is to be a Catholic; to deny it is to be a sectarian. Yet it can never be felt so long as we confound those inward experiences, which are the substance of faith, with their outward doctrinal and institutional expressions, and try to see in these latter the embryonic forms of Christian dogma and observance. "It is the spirit that quickeneth, the flesh profiteth nothing." It is in the inward experiences, not in their outward manifestations, that the parentage of religions is to be sought. Here, undoubtedly, the *Programme* penetrates the deeper and better mind of Christian Catholicism in a way that was hardly possible for scholastic theology with its narrow aprioristic outlook upon history. If no man can come to the Father but through Christ, if there is no other Name given under Heaven through which men may be saved, yet Christ is an ineffable Spirit who, under a thousand ever unworthy names, strives ceaselessly with every human soul and conscience, however ignorant of His historical manifestation as Jesus of Nazareth.

If, then, Modernism opens a possible way to a more or less explicit unity of spirit, and even uniformity of expression, among the severed branches of Christendom, it acknowledges among all the religions of the world a certain unity in variety as of many mansions in the House of the Universal Father. He who is scandalised at this would have been scandalised at Christ.

But though this movement in the Roman Church towards a higher and truer expression of Catholicism interests religion directly, it is also inspired by a wider and deeper interest to which that of the various religious institutions is subservient; and its bearings on public life and civilisation, if more remote, are not less important and not less real. It is now many years since one of our leading sociologists pointed out the disaster threatening a civilisation entrusted solely to the competing forces of man's self-regarding instincts, unchecked and unqualified by those altruistic self-sacrificing ideals for which a practical and theoretical materialism finds no room or justification. It is manifest that selfishness is not less, but even more, effectual than selflessness in setting man's wits to work in its service, and that it can build up a civilisation that tends to become a veritable Kingdom of Self or Kingdom of Satan. But such a civilisation is essentially parasitic; and, if wholly victorious over its host, must prey upon itself and come to nought. It is idle to invoke religion, with its sanction of altruism, as a mere social expedient, if religion be not true, or be no more than a useful illusion. Grown men cannot be kept in order by the bogies of their infancy. Tell them that their altruistic and humanitarian instincts, feebler, though not less real, than their egoism, are but tricks of crafty Nature for her own ends, and they will fight Nature as they fight one another—but to their destruction.

The new attempts to civilise and govern on a secularist basis do not promise well. To all appearance we are being hurried to anarchy and disruption. Each man's faith is in the faith of the rest; none dare say, in his own strength, "I see, I believe, I hope." Heretofore nations have risen and triumphed through common intuitions, beliefs, and aims that were at root religious—the products of some sort of faith. As this seems no longer possible, it is proposed to unite them by the free play and eventual equilibrium of those disruptive instincts which faith had formerly held in check, or utilised only as servile forces in the interests of the common good. Now "servants rule over us, and there is none that doth deliver us out of their hand." Cavour's policy of "a free Church in a free State" was in reality a policy of despair—an abdication of right on the part of the State in answer to the Church's violation of right.

In so far as they have adopted this policy, modern governments have discrowned themselves and let the sceptre pass from their hands. He was a wise man who said: "Let me make the nation's songs, and let who will make its laws." Still more important than laws or songs is the inspiring power of religion, the deepest and strongest educational force.

What has necessitated this secularisation of governments, and the consequent materialistic view of authority, is to a great extent the disruption of Christendom into a number of conflicting sects, each attaching a divine authority to its own dogmatic and institutional peculiarities, each regarding the defence of such peculiarities as the highest of all duties and resenting State interference as sacrilege. So long as one form of Christianity was practically predominant and without any serious competitor a State religion was no public injustice. But when this ceased to be the case the simplest expedient was for the State to assume an attitude of indifference and to allow the sects to settle their own disputes. A graver cause, especially in Latin countries, has been the habitual identification of religion with so much that is repugnant to modern ideas—political, social, moral, philosophical, scientific, historical; with so much that is simply obstructive of the democratic and scientific movements which are the main characteristics of our age. So fatally has the Roman Church entangled the cause of Christ with its mediæval expression, with forms, once life-giving but now obsolete and socially pestilential, that the whole plexus of substance and form has been thrust aside violently and indiscriminately by the long-repressed forces of progress and expansion. When the Latin Church points with ill-concealed satisfaction to the embarrassments created for secularist governments by a godless freemasonry or by an anti-religious socialism; when she draws thence a moral as to her own indispensableness, she would do well to remember how largely the responsibility for this chaos and anarchy lies at her own door. Instead, she offers these governments the alternative of restoring her mediæval theocracy, or of having all her religious influence used for their overthrow.

Yet nothing is more baseless or suicidal than this revolt of the modern world against Christ. Where is there anything good or true or lasting in its inspirations that it does not owe to Him? Who was it that taught us to take the side of the downtrodden multitudes against their spiritual and temporal oppressors? Who was it that set before us the true ideals of liberty, fraternity, and equality? Who was it that destroyed the preposterous claims of absolutism and taught us to obey God rather than man? Who was it that made truth the heritage of the crowd and not the monopoly of a clerical caste? Who swept away the magisterial in favour of a ministerial ideal of government in Church and State? Who was it that came to put down the mighty from their seat and to exalt the humble and meek; to fill the hungry and send the rich empty away? Who was it that not only lived, but died for these principles, and did so formally as an incarnate manifestation of the Divine Will? Is it not precisely the worship of Christ as God, the confession of His Gospel as the Will of God, that has given these principles of truth and liberty a vigour which has enabled them to struggle these two thousand years with the spirit of paganism, ever seeking, both in Church and State, to subdue them to its own selfish ends? And alas! with such success that Christ may be called that unknown God which the secularised world of to-day ignorantly worships.

We can, however, conceive a very changed aspect of affairs if the Roman Church should ever come to accept the *Programme of Modernism;* if she should ever cease to claim divine origin and immutability for the governmental forms, the intellectual formulas, in which her faith-experiences found suitable expression in an earlier age, and should adopt, not as of absolute but as of relative value, those of the rapidly-changing times; if she were to offer her spiritual services to civilisation, not in favour of the contingencies of political and social theories or of philosophical and scientific opinions, but in support of those eternal and unchanging principles of the Gospel which are and have been the inspiration and motive power of our progress towards light and liberty. Still more would the Catholic doctrine of a relative though unequal value in all religions, if rightly expressed and understood, do much to soften the asperities of the religious problem in countries where warring creeds now trouble the public peace and force governments into an ostentatious indifferentism that is practically atheistic.

For although modern conditions will ever forbid governments to appropriate this creed or that, there is no reason why they should not display a practical veneration for every religion, so far as it inculcates those vital and pre-eminently Christian principles which are the nerve, bone, and muscle of public life, and so far as it lends them the authority of a divine origin and a divine sanction. It is rather the ethical fruits of religion than its other-world theories and constructions that are of direct interest to the public weal. But an absolute morality, an ethic divorced from religion, has never yet knit a people together. Morality, to that end, must have a mystical, other-world basis, however diverse the symbols under which it is conceived and expressed. With the nature of this symbolism the State need not concern itself. All its care need be that the moral principles necessary for a healthy and vigorous public life should have their roots in eternity and their sanction in the Will that rules the world—in the public conscience recognised as the voice of God. As long as any religion gives such supernatural sanction to the great Christian principles of self-renunciation, self-mastery, devotion to the divine cause of truth and justice and liberty, to all that is meant by the Kingdom of God upon earth; as long as its ethical and social fruits are not enervating and decadent, such a religion, whatever its theology, deserves not merely liberty and toleration, but active support and protection as co-operating with the State for the public good. But if religions will step out of their bounds and claim divine jurisdiction in the foreign realms of politics and science; if their rivalries with one another over such matters, raised to points of faith, make them sources of social disunion and rancour, then the present miserable conditions will only go from bad to worse, and Church and State will continue to diverge, to their mutual impoverishment and destruction.

There should be no question of the State being under the Churches, or of the Churches under the State. This is analogous to the false dilemma that arises when Faith is identified with its contingent theological expression, and we are asked: Is theology to be subject to the other sciences, or are they to be subject to theology? The latter, surely, if theology be the revealed Word of God. But if it be only the scientific and human expression of that Word, the dilemma ceases. No science is to be subject to its fellow, but all are subject together to experience and to the general principles of science. Similarly, if the institutions and laws and officers of the Church are divine, the State must surely be subject to the Church. But if they are only representative of the divine, then both State and Church together are subject to an end, and a good which is higher than either apart, and which requires both of them for its embodiment, expression, and service. However inarticulately, the *Programme of Modernism* endeavours to give utterance to ideas of this kind that are stirring in the hearts of those who are partisans neither of Church nor of State, but of the common good of humanity, to which both are but instrumental.

If the official Church of Rome almost necessarily turns a deaf ear to a call for such costing self-renunciation, yet all the living fibres of her vast organism vibrate responsively to that voice that first called her into existence, and now calls her to wake from dreams of a dead past to the reality of a living present.

Authority, gradually gathered into the hands of a few who will not easily suffer themselves to be dispossessed, will be all for the *status quo*. Yet pressure from without, as in the past it has modified, so in the near future may utterly nullify, the opposition offered by authority to the spontaneous development of the deeper Catholicism. Already there is a strong suggestion of despair in the blind, self-defeating violence of its opposition to the forces that make for the life of the Church and threaten to burst her bonds asunder. We seem to be witnessing the last convulsions of absolutism in its death-agony. It is hard not to see the hand of an all-over-ruling Providence in the way that the deepest desires of the reigning Pontiff—of whose evangelical spirit there need be no doubt—are being furthered by the very defeat of the measures which he has taken for their realisation; how the unwise counsels he has received from far less worthy men have either been brought to nought or have produced results which must seem to him disastrous. It is the deepest desire of our heart that always prevails with Heaven, not our faulty interpretation and utterance of it, nor our misdirected efforts for its fulfilment. The hearts of popes, as of kings, are in the hand of the Lord, and He turns them whither He will.

In conclusion, there are two documents within the covers of this little volume, each the manifestation of a spirit, each purporting to be the true interpretation of Catholic Christianity. Apart from the detailed examination of their arguments we should attend to their cumulative appeal, not merely to the mind but to the heart and the religious sense. In each case let us ask ourselves: What manner of spirit is this? A spirit of light or of darkness; of peace or of strife; of sweetness or of bitterness; of gentleness or of violence; of comprehension or of exclusiveness? Whose voice do we hear? "He that heareth you, heareth Me," are words that have often received a strangely harsh and juridical interpretation. They mean that those only who speak as Christ spoke speak in His name; and that those who have once heard His voice will recognise it when they hear it again, and will obey it with that absolute obedience due to spiritual authority alone—to the appeal of Truth to the mind, and of Goodness to the conscience, and of Love to the heart.

A. L. L.

LONDON, *December* 27, 1907.

# CONTENTS

# The Programme of Modernism

## NEED OF AN EXPLANATION

A DOCUMENT so weighty, both in substance and form, as the Encyclical which we have reproduced at the end of this book; an attempt so deliberate to present "Modernist" * views to the public under a false and unfavourable light; a condemnation so authoritative of us Modernists as dangerous foes of Christian piety and unconscious promoters of atheism, make it a duty, which we owe to our own conscience, to the collective conscience, of the faithful, and to an anxious and expectant public, to lay bare our whole mind without reserve or concealment. We cannot possibly remain silent under the violent accusation which the chief authority of the Church, albeit recognising us as her faith-

* Let us say, once and for all, that we use this term only that we may be understood by those who have learnt it from the Encyclical, and that we do not need a new name to describe an attitude which we consider to be simply that of Christians and Catholics who live in harmony with the spirit of their day.

ful subjects and as resolved to cling to her till our last breath, heaps upon our head. Hence there is nothing arrogant in our reply, since it is an elementary principle of justice for those who are accused to defend themselves; nor can we believe that this right has been taken from us at a moment so critical for the fortunes of Catholic Christianity. And this all the more that if the Encyclical, with unwonted harshness, has struck us with a peremptory condemnation, it has also chosen, by a procedure for which we are most grateful, to set forth our opinions in its own fashion and to precede its verdict by a somewhat facile refutation of them. On this account we are led to hold that verdict for a valid one only just so far as the synthesis of our position contained in the Encyclical is exact, and so far as the reasons arrayed against us in the name of tradition are solid. It is therefore not only our right but our duty to intervene, to expose the unfair attack which the Encyclical seems to make upon us, and to examine the teachings for which we are rebuked. Devoted sons of the Church, obedient to that authority in which we recognise a continuation of the apostolic pastoral ministry, aware of the harmony which in every religious society should govern the relations between the rulers and the individual conscience, sharers in that intense spiritual life which pervades all the members of the Catholic community which is the mystical body of Christ, we present ourselves without any disrespect, but with a profound sense of the rights of our religious personality, before the tribunal of the community to which we belong to answer the accusations alleged against us. We do not offer excuses, still less are we going to beg pardon as offenders; we simply set forth our position and invite the judgment of our brethren upon it, and indeed the judgment of history. At this moment, pregnant with all sorts of moral revolution, when the intellectual world, still alienated from Christ and his Church, progresses in a hundred ways towards some indefinable renewal of spirit, we ask ourselves frankly: Is there in the Catholic Church—in that great organism in which the religious spirit of the Gospel has come to embody itself—is there a power of conquest or simply a conservative instinct? Does she still hide in the secret complexities of her wonderful organisation capacities for winning adherents, or is her vitality threatened by the germs of a speedy decay? Is her mission henceforth to be limited to a suspicious vigilance over the rude and simple faith of her rapidly-dwindling followers, or will she rouse herself to the reacquisition of that social influence which she has lost through long years of listless self-isolation? For ourselves, we have long since answered this critical question. We have ever watched the aspirations of the contemporary mind with sympathetic interest; our hearts have beaten in unison with its glowing enthusiasm for the new ideals of universal brotherhood; and we have seen in all its movements the symptoms of a glorious revival of religion. Spontaneously the word of Christ has risen to our lips: "Behold the fields are white unto the harvest! Lift up your heads for your redemption draweth nigh." Speaking the language of our age, and thinking its thought, we have tried to bring it into touch with the teachings of Catholicism, that through such contact their profound mutual affinities might be made evident. We cannot believe that the Church will ultimately reject our programme as mischievous. We may well have made mistakes in some of our conciliatory attempts; in which case we desire nothing better than charitable correction. But this is no reason for passing a sharp and peremptory condemnation on the whole of a work which has cost so much sacrifice and self-denial.

If the Church has not lost all sense of her Catholic destiny, if in the depths of her soul there still reverberates some echo of the prophecy, "There shall be one fold and one shepherd," she should break forth from the narrow confines of her deserted sanctuary, no longer visited by the warmth of that public life which throbs alike in the workshop and the university; she should try to get into touch with men, to find the way to their consciences, to kill the distrust of her bred in them by aloofness and misunderstanding. It is a question of reviving a piety that has been perverted, of seeking in the depths of the interior life the buried, but not extinguished, sparks of the ancient spirit of Christianity, of insisting on those ideals which govern the activity of the world of to-day and which are Christian in substance—that sense of altruism, that desire of sacrifice, which only the Gospel can infuse—in short, of uniting the scattered fragments of Christendom in some higher expression of that religious hope which is the sum and substance of the teaching of Jesus. But the Church and Society can never meet on the basis of those ideas which prevailed at the Council of Trent, nor can they converse together in mediæval language. How many days have dawned since the time of Innocent III.! How many events have ripened since those of Paul III.! Philosophy and religious thought which grow with the growth of the general mind, present to-day a very different aspect from any which the monks of the mediæval universities or the apologists of the counter-Reformation could possibly have foreseen. What wonder then that the old dogmatic formularies sound unintelligible to our contemporaries, or that the traditional theocratic pretensions shock their most elementary sense of personal responsibility? The general, like the individual, consciousness never passes through two perfectly similar moments in its history. As every impression and external event writes itself in the spirit, and by enriching it transforms it into something new, so the collective mind and sentiments are continually transformed by the course of history. To exist is to change. Whence it is clear that it is impossible to impose religious experience on the modern mind in the same forms as were adapted to the utterly different mediæval mind. The Church cannot, and ought not to, pretend that the *Summa* of Aquinas answers to the exigencies of religious thought in the twentieth century. The amorphous theology of the Carlovingian days proved insufficient to the university requirements of the thirteenth century. The theories of the Pauline literature were revised and transformed by the platonising fathers of the third and fourth centuries. Nor, on the other hand, should the Church be fearful, as though the venerable religious traditions of which she is the jealous guardian were now incapable of any vital adaptation. What was possible in the past is possible to-day, and will be always possible. The religion of Christ, which is simply a spirit of hope in the triumph of the divine kingdom of righteousness, is susceptible of any theoretical restatement that rests on idealistic presuppositions. And such presuppositions are common to the new tendencies of current philosophy which the Church therefore can embrace with a secure conscience, quickening it with the lofty aspirations fostered by the Gospel. Authority, therefore, should not condemn *a priori* this labour of synthesis enthusiastically inaugurated by so many high-minded thinkers.

The Encyclical reproaches us with pride and obstinacy. We would fain search our hearts for the most fervid utterance of our Christian feeling and say to Pius X.: "Holy Father, as becomes your devoted sons, we can assure you in all frankness and sincerity that our work is untainted by any sort of vain desire of praise. We have passed through long periods of anguish when, on leaving our Catholic schools or seminaries, with our minds full of scholastic teaching, we have little by little grown familiar with the culture of our own times and have felt the solidity of that theoretical ground which we had learnt to regard as the indisputable basis of Catholic faith give way beneath our feet. By prayer and by study we have sought light from on high, and this light has been created in our souls. The pretended bases of faith have proved themselves rotten beyond cure. But the faith itself, that rich heritage of Catholic religious experience, we have felt beating with a new life within our hearts, and we have seen unmistakably its perfect consistence with the best exigencies of contemporary thought. We have girt ourselves to the task of spreading to those round us this new experience of Catholicism whose possibilities of success we have discerned. Do not repulse us, Holy Father! our efforts may fail, but our programme is vital, nor is there any other way for the Church to succeed."

This is what we would say to him who embodies the teaching authority of the Church. Shall we then be regarded as rebels? It is possible.

Through a series of causes into which we need not here enter, Catholics seem to have lost every elementary sense of responsibility and personal dignity. Instead of being met with a service of reasonable and therefore discerning obedience, the acts of their supreme rulers are received with the unconscious acquiescence of irresponsible beings. This reacts unfavourably on the exercise of authority itself which loses sight of its proper limits and its true function, and transforms itself into an absolutism inconsistent with that reasonable spiritual government instituted by Christ "in whom we have passed from servitude to freedom."

Hence, whatever may at first be thought of our conduct, we believe we are rendering a true service to the Church in breaking through this deplorable tradition of abuses and concessions, and in respectfully but firmly explaining our contentions, which have been condemned only because so little understood by those in power. And in this we shall only be following the lead of some of the Church's noblest children, who in similar crises never hesitated to come to the aid of authority with their loyal warnings and reproaches. That this may not seem mere assertion, let us call to mind the words addressed to Pope Boniface IV. by the great Irish saint, Columbanus, founder of the monastery of Bobbio. At the beginning of the seventh century Italy was in a state of veritable religious anarchy. The so-called question of the three Chapters divided clergy and laity into a host of conflicting parties, each of which, being preoccupied with domestic controversies, was utterly indifferent to the conversion of the Arians, with whom Lombardy was infested. The Papacy itself, aware of the weakness of Vigilius, did not dare to meddle in so serious a dispute or to use its authority to command peace. Slanderous rumours were circulated as to the orthodoxy of Boniface IV., who had not courage to speak out and repel the calumny. It was necessary to shake Rome out of her torpor, and to point out to the Pope the only way to secure peace. From his monastery Columbanus boldly wrote:* "God's cause is in danger; I will not fear what men may say. When necessity urges we must give no ear to the suggestions of timidity and weakness. Listen then, Holy Father, to the suggestions of a loving heart and loyal soul. Whatever I say

* Ep. v. M.P.L. 80.

that is useful and right will all redound to your honour, for does not the wisdom of the scholars bring glory to their teacher? But should any unseasonable words escape me, put them down not to my pride but to my indiscretion. Behold, Father, how the billows rage, how the waves fill the ship, and the ship is in peril! And the fault is yours, if you have done wrong. Your sons do right to resist you, to hold no further communion with you till the memory of the wicked be rooted out and consigned to oblivion. If all they say is true, your sons are at the head and you are at the tail, and sorry I am to have to say so. They, therefore, shall be your judges (albeit your sons) who have always remained true to the faith. And so the more you are honoured by the dignity of your position, so much the more are you most undoubtedly bound to take all precautions lest your power suffer shipwreck through any fault of your own. You will keep that power in your hands just so long as your conscience is straight. He alone is the faithful doorkeeper of God's kingdom who, holding the true doctrine, knows how to let in the worthy and keep out the unworthy. Although we all know how Christ trusted Peter with the keys (on the strength of which fact you claim I know not what proud privileges of authority over others), yet remember your power will decrease before God if you forget the duties it entails."

Thus have saints spoken in the face of Peter, not because they deemed themselves saints, but because they were sensible of those duties common to all loyal sons of the Church, be they saints or sinners. Following such examples, which we might easily multiply, and all-conscious of our shortcomings in respect to sanctity, we would say to Pius X.: "Give ear to us, Holy Father. We propose to you a method which has already shown itself useful in regaining that spiritual power in the world which the Church has so pitiably forfeited. Before you reject us, before you solemnly bury yourself away in mediæval dreams of a political and intellectual theocracy, think for a moment on your responsibility to God, to society, to history, and consider carefully whether your policy of a return to the past may not end in sterilising the Church of which you are in charge."

# EXPLANATION OF THE MODERNIST SYSTEM

## SEC. I.—NOT PHILOSOPHY BUT CRITICISM THE PRESUPPOSITION OF MODERNISM

FIRST of all we must lay bare an equivocation by which inexpert readers of the Encyclical might easily be misled. That document starts with the assumption that there lies at the root of Modernism a certain philosophical system from which we deduce our critical methods, whether biblical or historical; in other words, that our zeal to reconcile the doctrines of Catholic tradition with the conclusions of positive science springs really from some theoretical apriorism which we defend through our ignorance of scholasticism and the rebellious pride of our reason. Now the assertion is false, and since it is the basis on which the Encyclical arranges its various arguments we cannot in our reply follow the order of that fallacious arrangement; but we must first of all show the utter emptiness of this allegation, and then discuss the theories which the Encyclical imputes to us.

In truth, the historical development, the methods

and programme of so-called Modernism are very different from what they are said to be by the compilers of *Pascendi Gregis.*

So far from our philosophy dictating our critical method, it is the critical method that has, of its own accord, forced us to a very tentative and uncertain formulation of various philosophical conclusions, or better still, to a clearer exposition of certain ways of thinking to which Catholic apologetic has never been wholly a stranger. This independence of our criticism in respect to our purely tentative philosophy is evident in many ways.

First of all, of their own nature, textual criticism, as well as the so-called Higher Criticism (that is, the internal analysis of biblical documents with a view to establishing their origin and value), prescind entirely from philosophical assumptions. A single luminous example will suffice—that furnished by the question of the *Comma Johanneum*—now settled for ever. In past days when theologians wanted to prove the doctrine of the Trinity they never omitted to quote from the Vulgate (1 John v. 7): "There are three that bear record *in Heaven, the Father, the Word, and the Holy Ghost.*" Now the italicised words are lacking in all the Greek MSS. of to-day, cursive or uncial, and in all the Greek epistolaries and lectionaries, and in all the ancient translations, except the Vulgate, in the works of the Greek Fathers and of other Greek writers prior to the twelfth century, in those of all the ancient Syrian and Armenian writers, and in those of a great number of the Latin Fathers. This silence of East and West is all the more remarkable as the passage would have been of priceless value in the Arian controversy. That it was not then appealed to, proves that it did not exist at the beginning of the fourth century. Moreover, a collation of MSS. and their comparison with the works of the heretic Priscillian, discovered a few years ago, makes it clear that the verse in question comes from Spain, and was fabricated by that heretic (A.D. 384) in favour of his trinitarian views, of which Peregrinus made himself the propagandist. Now it is plain that in order to arrive at such a conclusion and to study such a literary problem critically, no sort of philosophical doctrine or presupposition is required. The same can be said of a whole host of biblical and historical problems whose impartial solutions, leading to results so different from those of traditional Catholic criticism, are the true cause of that revolution in religious apologetic which we find forced upon us by sheer necessity. Does one really need any special philosophical preparation to trace a diversity of sources in the Pentateuch, or to convince oneself, by the most superficial comparison of texts, that the Fourth Gospel is a substantially different kind of work from the synoptics, or that the Nicene Creed is essentially a development of the Apostles' Creed?

But besides these intrinsic reasons, we can invoke indisputable facts in proof of the independence of our criticism in relation to our philosophical tendencies.

First of all, this criticism is far more ancient than the philosophy with which we are credited. Nothing had been heard of "agnosticism" or "immanentism" when between 1670 and 1690 Richard Simon published his marvellous *Histoires Critiques* of the Old and New Testament, which represents the first really serious application of scientific methods to the study of the documentary records of Catholic Revelation. The first of the two volumes, in particular, is at once a splendid scientific reconstruction of the literary history of the Israelites founded on a minute examination of the state of the texts that have gone to the compilation of the Bible and also an admirable treatise on the critical classification of the versions of the Hebrew text, with a list of the varieties of interpretations which it has received at different periods.

Nothing had been heard of "symbolism" or of historical "transfiguration" when Dr. J. Astruc, in an anonymous work published at Brussels 1753, "Conjectures sur les mémoires originaux dont il paraît que Moïse s'est servi pour composer le livre de la Genèse," tried for the first time to systematise the theory of the most ancient source used in that part of the Pentateuch.

Since the time of those great men, criticism, without the slightest vestige of philosophic preoccupation, has applied to the Bible and to the history of Christianity those very same scientific principles which indeed are not susceptive of any change or perversion for the simple reason that they are the principles of historical science as such. We are not to blame if, arriving on the scene after centuries of critical study, we find all those positions destroyed which traditional theology had assumed without discussing the texts or making sure of their documentary value; on the contrary, we think we deserve well of religious apologetic if we honestly strive to transfer the rational defence of faith from the tottering basis of what has proved to be an anti-critical exegesis, to the solid, because unassailable, basis offered by the deepest exigencies of the human soul and by those spiritual life-needs which have given birth to the whole process of Christianity.

Furthermore, the independence and priority of criticism in relation to philosophy in our intellectual movement can be established clearly in the case of more than one of our representative students. It was his long critical researches as to the Old and New Testament that led Abbé Loisy, whose former work had been exclusively critical, to write his celebrated studies (in 1900 and 1901) on *Revelation* and on *The Religion of Israel*, which were the beginning of his apologetic labours. It has been a prolonged documentary study of the Gospel narratives that has led so many of us to revise the traditional opinions about the foundation of the Church and the institution of the Sacraments.

Finally, it has been long years passed in the patient comparison of the various stages that mark the development of Catholic thought that have almost unconsciously driven us to adopt a new theory as to the development of dogma from the teaching of Christ, preferring to see everywhere the continual and secret working of a divine indwelling spirit rather than contradict plain facts by admitting an abrupt and complete revelation of the *Credo* which never took place. This is so true that some of us, who are constitutionally averse to synthetic efforts and impatient of every attempt at apologetic conciliation, avow ourselves critics pure and simple, ignoring, if not actually opposing, any tentative hypothesis to harmonise an unchanging faith with a progressive critical science.

We seem to have said enough to show that it is not an impartial estimate of facts but a clever polemical stratagem that leads the authors of the Encyclical to strike at what they suppose to be certain philosophical presuppositions of our system, but what are in any case the conclusions of long critical efforts and not the premisses nor the directing principles of the research by which those conclusions were reached. Hence we cannot, still less should we desire to, follow the Encyclical on to a ground so treacherous and insecure. No doubt it was a very convenient artifice to present our movement to the public as hingeing on a few abstract principles (how sorely distorted we shall presently see) whose designed paradoxical form makes them glaringly incompatible with the fundamental positions of Catholic theology. But it would be folly on our part to let such an equivocation pass without protest. We must rather vindicate before all things the critical basis and fundamental facts on which our whole system rests; we must show that if Modernism is not merely an empty or ambiguous term it stands for a method, or rather for *the* critical method, applied conscientiously to the religious forms of humanity in general, and to Catholicism in particular. And if such a faithful application leads to a complete revision of the positive bases on which the scholastic interpretation of Catholicism was raised, and so provokes the need of a new apology for our faith, this is not due to a freakish caprice of our reason, proudly contemptuous of scholasticism, whose principles, on the contrary, we understand very well and whose historical function we appreciate. It is due to a manifest exigence of the religious sense which seeks to preserve its power over men in ever new forms of thought. It was inevitable that mediæval scholasticism (*i. e.*, the fusion of Aristotelian thought with Catholic teaching such as it was up to the end of the twefth century) springing into existence in a period void of the least vestige of historic sense and of the remotest suspicion as to what had been the actual facts of the evolution of Christianity—it was inevitable that such a system should fall to pieces as soon as its presupposition of a mechanical revelation, petrified in the moment of its instantaneous completion, was found to be based on biblical and patristic texts accepted without any sense of critical discernment. Add to this, the criticism to which the logical realism of Aristotle has been subjected by the more recent philosophical tradition, and it is easy to imagine the disastrous crisis which has arisen for the scholastic interpretation of Catholicism. Modernism has been born and matured by the need of meeting this lamentable crisis, and it will continue to bear this party-name till the day when, after having created and propagated this new interpretation of Catholicism by force of its tenacious devotedness, it will mingle with, and become one and the same thing as, Catholicism.

The reasons are clear, then, why we do not think

fit to follow the Encyclical line by line in the deceptive picture it draws of the Modernist as philosopher, believer, theologian, critic, apologist, reformer, and to set over against each head of its accusation the sincere explanation of our modest aims and our true ideas. To us it seems a strange pretension to present Modernism as a synthesis, since we are the first to declare openly and emphatically that we have as yet no definite synthesis and are only groping our way laboriously, and with much hesitation, from the now assured results of criticism to some sort of apologetic, whose aim is not to subvert tradition but solely to make use of the eternal postulates of religion familiar to the most authentic conception of Catholicism.

We shall therefore put together briefly the results of biblical and historical criticism; we shall show how they have simply necessitated a change in our conception of inspiration and of revelation, and the introduction of the conception of religious evolution; how, as regards the New Testament, they have necessitated a distinction between the outward history and the inward history, between the historical Christ and the mystical Christ, the Christ of reason and the Christ of faith; we shall call attention to the undeniable fact that the Catholic tradition (that is, the living transmission of the religious spirit liberated by the Gospel) has undergone profound revolutions in respect to its theoretic formulation, beginning with the Messianic preachings of Christ and going on to the Hellenistic Fathers of the second century; thence, to the anti-Gnostic controversialists; thence to the definitions of the first ecumenical councils, to the mediæval doctors, to the scholastic systematisation, to the Tridentine formulas. And from this we shall show how the honest recognition of such an evolution has led us to justify our faith by the notion of the permanence of something divine in the life of the Church, in virtue whereof every new doctrinal formulation, every new juridical institution (in so far as it more or less consciously tends to the preservation of the Gospel spirit) can claim a divine origin and a divine maintenance.

No one can evade the results of scientific history, and so we shall start from them. Modern criticism has revolutionised the historical outlook; its method has become a most delicate and complex instrument on which alone we can depend if our evocation of the buried past is not to be mere fiction or romance. In applying this method to religious documents and tradition we are only logically consistent. Besides, we are thus only obeying an orthodox postulate of theology which puts the sacred Scriptures first among the *loci theologici* (that is, the source from which the teachings of faith can be drawn), and which demands that the Scriptures be so seriously and carefully studied that the structure reared upon them may not rest upon sand. When it is objected that Catholics prove the authority of the Church from Scripture, and the authority of Scripture from the Church, our approved apologists answer rightly that, in the former case, we argue from Scripture not as divinely inspired but as from a human document subject to the same canons of criticism as the Koran or the Homeric poems.

As S. Thomas* says, faith and reason cannot be in conflict. We should therefore courageously apply our criticism to the study of religion, confident that whatever is destroyed by the process can in no way belong to the substance of our religious faith.

Then when we come to discuss the philosophical principles for which the Encyclical rebukes us, we shall make it clear that some of the charges are simply false, and that if others are partly true they are nowise contrary to Catholic tradition, which, be it remembered, reaches back further than the *Summa* of S. Thomas, let alone the Council of Trent. Christianity had lived long before one or the other, and there is no reason why we should not uphold an interpretation of Catholicism older than either, if the circumstances that called for it were in some way analogous to those of the modern religious world.

---

* *Contra Gentiles*, i. 7.

### (*a*) *The Literary Criticism of the Old Testament*

The Encyclical marks it as a piece of cunning astuteness on the part of the Modernists that they disclaim to be philosophers in their dealings with history, whereas their history and criticism is mere philosophising from beginning to end. And indeed the critico-historical system which it fathers on them is a strictly aprioristic system in which facts are deduced from certain principles that are supposed to be the very pith and marrow of Modernism. There should have been some attempt to show that such is actually the method adopted and practised by Modernists. But the Encyclical passes over the point lightly, saying that "this is evident on a moment's reflection"—as though what we think could be ascertained by others on mere reflection. Not one word does it say as to the results reached by historical criticism, or as to the way in which they have, as a fact, been reached. Yet this is the very foundation of the inquiry from which we should begin. What the Encyclical has not done, let us try to do briefly.

The common and traditional notion is that in the Bible we possess an orderly and complete history of the revelation of the Old and New Testament, guaranteed true in every part by the authority of God, who, as He has inspired the Bible, may be called the principal historian; and also by the authority of the secondary historians, who were more or less immediate witnesses of the facts they record—such as Moses and Joshua for the Old Testament, Matthew, Mark, Luke, and John for the New. But this conception has been shaken to its foundations by literary criticism applied to the historical books of either Testament.

This began with the Pentateuch, commonly ascribed to Moses. Since the sixteenth century various critics have noticed reasons for denying the authorship of the Pentateuch, or at least of parts of it, to Moses, or even to the time of Moses. It was also observed that with the exception of certain parts, such as the Deuteronomic legislation, which expressly claim to be written by him, there is nothing in the book itself that points to his authorship.

But the full solution of the problem, not merely negative but positive, belongs to the nineteenth century and to that long series of illustrious critics who, by means of a most minute analysis applied to the Pentateuch from beginning to end, and after many tests and hypotheses, arrived unanimously at certain fixed conclusions. The upshot of their multitudinous observations may be reduced to the following heads: (1) All through the Pentateuch we find various *duplicates;* that is, narratives which record the same fact, or laws which refer to the same case; (2) Notwithstanding their similarity of content, these duplicates differ from one another palpably, not only in style but also in language, as shown by the constant use of certain words, and constructions and phrasings; (3) But they also differ in content, since in the narratives the same fact is often presented with different and mutually exclusive circumstances, or with the same circumstances in an inverted order; and in the laws, the precepts touching the same case are contradictory, sometimes in accidentals, sometimes even in substance; (4) But what is most to be noted is that the same matter is differently treated not only from an historical but from a religious point of view, whether as to the manner of conceiving God and His attributes, or as to that of conceiving the relations between God and man.

From the establishment of such facts we must necessarily infer that these duplicates cannot be the work of one and the same author, but demand different writers, not only on account of their resemblances (for it is not likely that an author should repeat himself in this way), but on account of their differences (since it is impossible that an author should contradict himself so openly at such brief intervals).

Criticism, however, is not contented with this negative result; it seeks to discover the nature and manner of the composition of the Pentateuch. It was first conjectured that the duplicates were separate fragments put together anyhow, so that the Pentateuch was merely a bundle of scraps. But later it became evident on deeper study that many of these fragments, while strikingly different in kind (and therefore in origin) in some cases, in others presented a no less striking resemblance, which made it possible to arrange two or more series of parallel fragments, each of which is characterised by certain linguistic, historical, juridical, and religious peculiarities. But that is not all. It was found that each series presented a well-ordered, and for the most part perfect, sequence. And all this, while on the one hand it has confirmed the former conclusion as to the diverse origin of the duplicates, has, on the other, furnished bases for the further conclusion that the Pentateuch is composed of originally separate documents, closely dove-tailed together by one or more redactors who had naturally to cut up, amplify and modify the said documents according as the unity or aim of their work demanded.

Leaving out of count a few brief fragments and editorial additions, the documents which form the Pentateuch are four: (1) That which was at first styled the Elohistic document, because it calls God Elohim up to the point where He reveals Himself to Moses as Jahve. But now it is known as the Priestly Code because, after a brief history of the world up to the death of Moses, it is wholly occupied with legislation concerning worship and priesthood. (2) Then there comes the "second Elohist" (now simply "the Elohist"), so-called because he prefers to speak of God as Elohim even after the Mosaic revelation. His work is mainly historical, beginning with the call of Abraham and ending with the death of Moses, but also embraces some legal scraps, notably that known as the Book of the Covenant (in Exodus), whose theme is mainly moral and religious. (3) The Javistic document, which is purely historical, beginning from the creation of the world, and which calls God Jahve throughout. (4) The Deuteronomist, so called because coinciding almost entirely with Deuteronomy. Like the Priestly Code it is principally a legal document, using history merely to illustrate and enforce the observance of the law, and ascribing the said history and law to Moses himself shortly before his death in the plain of Moab.

From what has been said it follows directly that the four documents which form the Pentateuch can neither be from the same author nor from the same period, since such different religious conceptions, and still more such different legal enactments, cannot belong to the same people at the same time: *Distingue tempora et conciliabis jura.*

At first it was thought that the four documents

might be chronologically arranged in the above order, the Priestly Code being the most ancient of all. But a closer criticism has dispelled this idea. A careful comparison with the other books of the Old Testament, historic and prophetic, shows that the legislation of the Priestly Code was, in its most salient points, unknown in Israel before the Babylonian captivity and only came into use later. Whence the conclusion that the document embodying the legislation was written after and not before the captivity; and since we are told that Esdras imposed on the new religious community of Jerusalem a law which he had brought from Babylon, it is natural to conclude that this was just the Priestly Code. Again, the epoch of the Deuteronomist can be fixed clearly enough, since its aim is to enforce the law (unknown to antiquity) of only one sanctuary for all Israel, and since it has been identified even by S. Jerome and other ancient ecclesiastical writers with the Book of the Law found in the reign of Josiah, and therefore composed not long before, and on the basis of which that pious king, having destroyed all the other sanctuaries of Palestine, decreed that Solomon's temple in Jerusalem should be the only lawful sanctuary for the Jews. The Elohist and Jahvist reach back to an earlier epoch, since they contain sacred ordinances which we find in use before the time of Josiah, and even from the most primitive times.

Those conclusions as to the origin of the several documents are strikingly confirmed by comparison with the prophetic writings. For we find that the Elohist and Jahvist documents agree in language and thought with the oldest prophets, like Amos and Hosea; the Deuteronomist with Jeremiah, who was contemporary with Josiah's reform; the Priestly Code with Ezekiel, who of all the prophets was most interested in the restoration of worship after the destruction of Jerusalem by the Chaldeans.

When we apply the same criticism to the other historical books of the Old Testament we see plainly that they are works of compilation and have not been written offhand. As for the Book of Joshua it is a continuation of the same documents out of which the Pentateuch is woven—a further proof that none of them can have been the work of Moses. If the sources of Judges and Kings are not the same as those of the Pentateuch, they derive from the same school of writers and have undergone a like process of editing. The Book of Chronicles, though a more recent compilation of more recent materials, is very important for our contention, since by using large and unacknowledged extracts from the Book of Kings it shows beyond doubt that the Jewish mode of compiling history was just what criticism infers and describes.

All this labour of critical construction is the work

not of Modernists but of eminent scientists of various nationalities and religions. Unless we are prepared to say that they are—what the Encyclical calls us Catholic critics—an international association of blusterers and impostors, their unanimous judgment must weigh even with those least versed in the difficult art of criticism. "Yes; but they are rationalists." What then? Their conclusions are not founded on their rationalism but on their reasons, on their vast knowledge, above all, on their conscientious investigation of texts and facts. Moreover, many of them are at one with us in their reverence for the divine authority of the Bible and in their recognition of Christ as their Saviour. Also those few Catholics who have devoted their lives and labours to these extensive and difficult studies have, often in spite of themselves, been plainly convinced of the legitimacy of biblical criticism. It is true that the Papal Commission, "De re biblica," in its famous answer of June 27, 1906, has solemnly declared that all the arguments amassed by criticism against the Mosaic authorship of the Pentateuch are nothing worth; but such a decree has not, and does not pretend to have, any scientific value.* It is well known that the more learned consultors of the

---

* By a recent *Motu Proprio* Pius X. declares the past and future decisions of that Commission to have the conscience-binding force of congregational decrees, *i. e.*, not scientific but juridical authority.

Commission, and those best known to the scientific world by their publications, all more or less accept the verdict of criticism. As for the theological consultors, who as usual cleave tenaciously to traditional opinions, one might say of each of them what Dr. Charles Briggs, the illustrious critic and philologist, well known for his Catholic tendencies, said of one of the secretaries of the Commission: "His treatment of the Bible is so unscientific, and his use of the Hebrew tongue exhibits such depths of ignorance that no expert could allow his right to any sort of opinion in the matter of Hebrew scholarship, and his very name is at once enough to discredit the answer of the Commission." * The philological and critical competence of the cardinals who had the decisive vote is on the same level; nor does their preoccupation with other affairs fit them to destroy with a hasty word the accumulated labours of so many generations of critics. It is as though they had been called on to decide by vote some intricate astronomical problem, as their predecessors were in the case of Galileo. It was quite natural that in order to get themselves out of their embarrassment they should hold fast to the argument from tradition. But the historical books of the Old Testament, from which they would prove such

* *The Papal Commission and the Pentateuch.* London: Longmans, 1900.

a continuous tradition from the time of Moses, have been submitted, as already said, to the same criticism as the Pentateuch itself, and when even the oldest of them speak of "the Law" they mean the Deuteronomic Law. The ascription of the entire Pentateuch to Moses occurs explicitly for the first time in the Book of Chronicles, written nearly a thousand years after Moses—an interval far too great to allow the tradition any historical value.

But while proclaiming aloud the insufficiency of the critical arguments, the Commission itself betrays a deep sense of their forcibleness. It is due to this sense that it admits that Moses may have employed secretaries whose writings he himself supervised and published. This is plainly a recognition of the composite character of the Pentateuch, a concession which cannot be defended in the form in which it is presented, and is, moreover, unequal to its purpose. For the diverse parts of the Pentateuch differ not only in form, so as to demand different writers, but also in content, so as to demand differently-instructed minds writing independently of one another and of any one directing editor. Also, to allow that in the course of time glosses and modifications have been introduced into the Pentateuch is to recognise that the critics are right when they say that certain passages bear on their faces the imprint of an age later than Moses. Yet here again the concession is not enough to save the Mosaic authorship, since many of the said passages bear no trace of being later than the main work, and harmonise perfectly with the general context, so that no calm and impartial critic could regard them as glosses.

In the face of such results of biblical criticism founded on undeniable facts, and allowed by all serious students who refuse to be biassed by prejudices inherited from the past, we Modernists cannot in conscience withdraw ourselves from the light of truth or put ourselves in harsh opposition to science and its leaders.

Rather, while on the one hand we honestly accept the assured results of criticism, we strive on the other so to modify our theology that criticism may not come in conflict with our faith.

Above all we have seen the necessity of abandoning the illusion that we possess in the Bible an orderly and complete history of the religion of Israel. The historical books of the Old Testament are compilations of documents belonging to different periods, each of which reflects back to the time of Moses or thereabouts the customs and institutions prevailing in its own day. Nevertheless they give us materials from which criticism can reconstruct the history of Israel, though they themselves do not reconstruct it for us.

Must we then say that the books of the Old Testament recount what is false? It is just here that we have to face the most delicate problem of reconciling faith and science without injury to the truth. We hold that no blame of untruthfulness can attach to the sacred authors. In point of fact "false" is a relative term. That a statement is false means not only that it is untrue to reality but that its author knows its untruth or wishes to impose it as true. Else we should have to say that Homer, Dante, Manzoni, and a host of writers were untruthful. Truth and falsehood must be estimated by the nature of the book and by the literary category to which it belongs. History, in the strict sense of the word looks to the exact reproduction of facts, whereas poetry and all other sorts of creative literature look to a different order of truth transcending the brute reality of facts. And these two kinds of literature are not divided by a deep and wide gulf. Midway between is to be found every degree of mixture of fact and imagination. There is also a sort of history which leaves more or less room for imaginary descriptions, speeches, and conversations. And this is the general manner of classical historians like Herodotus, Xenophon, Livy, and Tacitus, who are not therefore to be charged with untruthfulness. And so we ought not to wonder if orientals, naturally more enthusiastic and imaginative, mingle invention with history somewhat more liberally. We may not then settle the character of a book, even when written in narrative form, *a priori*, but only after a minute and careful examination. From such an examination it is evident that the narrative books of the Old Testament, compiled as they are with considerable freedom from different sources wherein the same facts are differently presented, are not histories in the strict and modern sense of the term. They may perhaps be called sacred histories, that is, histories compiled for and adapted to the development of religious life and feeling. Nor should every sort of invention be excluded from the idea of religious history for stories partly or wholly imaginary are often more edifying than rigorously-verified facts, and we rightly set great store by the old-world legends of the saints and draw great profit from them, though we know that they contain much that derives only from the devout imagination of the writer. In the Bible itself we have a palpable example of this harmless sort of fiction in the Book of Wisdom, which pretends to be the utterance of Solomon, whereas all the world knows now that it was written in Greek shortly before the Christian era. But the theologians have been so long accustomed to use the Bible as a basis for arguments and strict logical demonstrations that they necessarily imagine it must have been written to serve this dialectical purpose, which it could not do were it not free from every element of fiction. Yet this is mere prejudice. Examined carefully the historical books of the Old Testament do not make the least pretence to furnish intellectual arguments, but simply to purify the hearts of their readers. Nor are the legal portions an exception. As the author of Wisdom could ascribe his book to Solomon, because Solomon was possibly the inventor and most illustrious representative of the sapiential literature, so other authors could attribute various and successive legal codes to Moses because the Thorah—that is, the law-giving power in Israel—derived from Moses. The authority of a law, moreover, did not rest on its being written by Moses but on its antiquity or some such reason. So also Josiah, when he undertook a reformation on the basis of the Deuteronomic law, did not rest it on the Mosaic origin of the law but on the authority of the prophets then living, and on the fact that the system of many sanctuaries which it condemned had brought down upon Israel the divine chastisement therein threatened.

From all this it is plain in what sense we understand and admit that theory which justifies biblical errors as serving the interests of the spiritual life—a theory which the Encyclical reproaches us with. We do not allow that there are, strictly speaking, any errors in the Bible, still less any lies—not even lies of edification—and therefore we have no need to excuse them by the said theory. But the interests of religious life can explain the use of certain literary artifices in the Bible which do not correspond to the usages and needs of our day. It is owing just to these artifices and to the peculiar religious needs of the people for whom each of these books was written, that we so often fail to find what we should expect in the Bible and find what we should not expect.

In the second place, the results of criticism have forced us to abandon the old idea of biblical inspiration. Up to recent times inspiration was explained as a verbal dictation by the Holy Ghost. But in the latter half of the nineteenth century the scholastics themselves recognised that even a superficial examination of the Bible forbade the idea that the sacred writer was merely and wholly a passive instrument, and while they reserved to God the authorship of each and every idea contained in the book, they allowed that the verbal expression of those ideas might (in spite of the unanimous tradition to the contrary) be ascribed to the wit of man. But the results of criticism force us much further. As the words are not directly from God, so neither are the ideas, since they often clash with one another. The whole book, words and ideas alike, is the work of man without thereby ceasing to be wholly, as to both words and ideas—a distinction we can set aside as unknown to antiquity—the work of God. Inspiration can no longer be considered as the mechanical transmission of words or ideas from God to man, but as a vital conceiving of word and idea together on the part of man's spirit united in a special and supernatural manner to God, who thus in man, and by means of man, has raised the people of Israel to ever higher stages of religious development.

Hence it is easy to see how our notion of inspiration differs from that which the Encyclical ascribes to us. We do not consider inspiration to be simply the manifestation which every believer, by a sort of internal necessity, is compelled to make of his faith. We see in it a special work of God, nay more, the realisation of a divine and stupendous plan for the salvation of mankind. That there are in the sacred Scriptures mistakes not only of language and style but also of matter, is a fact that is given by observation and critical analysis. We have not invented this fact, but our mode of conceiving inspiration enables us to explain it. If God Himself had found the words and ideas, and had thus transmitted them mechanically to the sacred writers, He would surely have sought out those best suited to the capacity of all readers of all times; He would not have needed to repeat Himself in various and often contradictory ways. But since words and ideas are the work of man they are naturally subject to the imperfections of man, whence these repetitions and discords. Inspiration was not given to destroy such religiously-irrelevant imperfections, but that notwithstanding its imperfections the work of man should contribute each time a little more to the fulfilment of the divine plan of redemption.

Finally, criticism forces us to alter our notion, not only of inspiration but of revelation—not indeed substantially, for we hold that revelation is God's message to man, but as to the manner in which that message is transmitted to man. The Encyclical insists above all things on the external character of revelation. Nor do we ourselves deny that the transmission of the divine message to the faithful at large demands an external instrument, that is to say, the prophet or divine messenger who acts as intermediary between God and the community. But the question is as to how, in the first instance, the message is transmitted to the prophet or messenger. The biblical narratives present this transmission as external in form, as words directed to the bodily ear, or as visions beheld with the bodily eye. But does this pretend to be literal fact and not rather a literary device? The latter supposition, after all we have said about the veracity of sacred history, is certainly not impossible; nay, it seems the more probable if we consider that the same theophany (*e. g.*, that to Moses on Mount Sinai) has been quite differently described in different documents. It has been noticed that, generally speaking, the Jahvist gives objective reality to divine apparitions, that the Elohist describes them as visions during sleep, and that the Priestly Code reduces the sense-elements simply to that of the divine word—"The Lord said," etc. May it not be that these various presentments, progressively dematerialised, stand for a fact of the purely spiritual order?

At all events it is impossible to gather exactly from the historical books of the Old Testament what the nature of revelation really was; and we should rather turn to the prophetic books, which offer a more direct and safer guidance. Now if at times the prophets speak of visions, for the most part they do not allude to them and rather conceive the voice of God as an inward and irresistible compulsion. It is hard to see why such importance should be attached by the Encyclical to the externality of revelation as though it alone could make us certain that God had spoken to man, whereas everyone knows that God cannot be the direct object of external sensation, nor can He lack means to reveal Himself directly and unmistakably to the soul of His prophet. Sacred history presents revelation to us not as external, but as given once and for all by means of one man—Moses, in such wise that the prophets did no more than explain and inculcate the Mosaic revelation. But here again criticism has forced us to change our ideas. It has taught us that the various institutions and legislations have succeeded one another in the course of long ages, each changing and improving on the one before.

The historical books of the Old Testament afford a vista of an earlier epoch in which the children of Israel were on the same religious level as the other nations. At the time of each writer that level has been left behind, but not entirely; and it is plain that Israel still needs a continual providence on God's part to guard against a relapse into idolatry and uncleanness. The danger of such a relapse is felt to be more or less acute in the different historical books. In this great progressive work of the religious reform and elevation of Israel God has used the instrumentality not only of Moses, but also of his successors, the prophets, many of whose names, not to say writings, are lost to us. God's spirit is not tied to a single epoch or to a particular little group of persons, but is spread abroad over the ages and generations of humanity, ever furthering the perfection of his plan of redemption.

A last, but not least important, remark as to revelation. Its object has never been so much an abstract knowledge of the Divinity, as a practical instruction concerning the worship of God and the conforming of our lives to the supreme rule of his will. The prophets have given such guidance to kings and peoples in special emergencies; the Pentateuch deals with general cases; and the historical books recount the good and the evil that has befallen Israel according as the law has been observed or transgressed.

### (*b*) *Criticism and the New Testament*

The Gospels are for Christianity what the Pentateuch is for Israel. In the light of criticism there are also certain analogies between these the two most interesting parts of the Bible. As the origins of the religion of Israel are differently presented in the four documents woven into the Pentateuch, so are the origins of Christianity by the four Gospels, which however have been kept separate by the Church, and have not been woven into such a diatessaron as was used for a long time in the ancient Church of Syria.

And if we adhere to the letter, the differences between the Gospels in very many cases amount to real and unmistakable contradictions. Of these the Encyclical will hear nothing and, against the judgments of criticism, appeals with scorn to the innumerable series of Doctors and Fathers who, though far in a way more holy and learned than the Modernists, have found no such defects in the sacred writings. But in point of fact even the said Doctors, in reading and comparing the Gospels, have often noted glaring contradictions, which they have piously striven to explain away by putting the blame on a vitiated codex, or on an incompetent translator, or on the misapprehension of the reader. But has their ingenuity in establishing a perfect harmony between the Gospels ever really been successful? That is the question. The endless series of new Gospel harmonies and new attempts at conciliation seems to say, No. To take an example: How many explanations have been, and are daily, suggested to reconcile the first three Gospels with the fourth as to the date of the Last Supper and the death of Christ? This means that a solution of the contradiction clear enough to satisfy everyone cannot be found because it does not exist. But were it a question of this and a few other rare cases it would matter little. The truth is, however, that there is hardly a single portion of any consequence which is not marked by serious and insuperable divergences on the part of the first three Evangelists.

What the Encyclical says is partly true: there are divergences in the Gospels which were wholly unnoticed in past times; and therefore the Biblical Commission (in its decree, May 29, 1907—*De Auctore et veritate historica quarti Evangelii*) appeals in vain to the solution given in the past by the Fathers and by Catholic exegetes to difficulties suggested by a comparison of the Fourth Gospel with the synoptics. They could not solve difficulties of which they were unaware. Criticism has done for the Gospels what it has done for the Pentateuch. It has submitted each of them to a systematic examination and brought out its peculiar characteristics, and has thus been able to determine not only its particular differences from the other Gospels, but those general differences of scope and character on which these particular differences depend. By way of explanation let us take an example. It is noticeable that in the Gospel of S. Mark the life of Jesus follows an orderly and progressive development. At first His divine sonship is a secret revealed to Him alone by the Father at His baptism. Later, He works such miracles as only the Son of God could work, but deliberately refrains from claiming that title; forbids the devils to call Him by it; forbids those whom He cures to publish the miracle. The first to infer His Messiahship from His works is Simon Peter, who confesses his faith at Cæsarea. From that time forth Jesus often speaks of His Christhood and of the passion which it necessarily involves, but always in secret and only to His disciples. The crowd acknowledge and proclaim Him to be the Messiah for the first time at His solemn entrance into Jerusalem, and Jesus Himself first declares it openly in His trial before the Sanhedrin. Such is the trend of the second and oldest Gospel.

In Matthew and Luke, on the contrary, Jesus is presented to the public as the Son of God from the very beginning, at His baptism; and He Himself from the first—in the Sermon on the Mount (Matthew) and in the opening discourse at Nazareth (Luke)—comes forward publicly as the supreme lawgiver, the Lord, the Universal Judge, the Christ or the Anointed of God; and accordingly, long before the confession of Peter, His disciples call Him the Lord and the Son of God. And yet in spite of this, these two Evangelists retain the injunctions to the healed and to the devils not to declare Him, as well as the confession of Peter, to which S. Matthew attaches a particular importance. Also, the Fourth Gospel, like Matthew and Luke, makes John proclaim Jesus publicly to be the Son of God at His baptism and makes the disciples acknowledge Him as such from the first. But it goes further than the other two. Not only does it retain no trace of the scheme followed by S. Mark, no trace of Jesus' injunctions to silence, or even of the confession of S. Peter, but besides all this it represents Jesus as, from the first, speaking of nothing but Himself, declaring His divine prerogatives and defending them against the attacks of the Jews—His heavenly origin, His priority to the world, His unity with the Father, His co-operation in the work of creation and revelation, etc.,—ideas, not one of which is to be met with in the other Gospels and which the Evangelist has first set forth in his prologue and has, in part, put into the mouth of John the Baptist.

Corresponding to this way of conceiving Jesus' revelation of His divine sonship, is the way in which his story is told so as to illustrate that sonship. Mark deprives the humanity of Jesus of none of its traits. He ascribes to Him pity, tenderness, anger, impatience, fear, weariness, and even temptation; a limited power, as when at Capernaum He cured many but not all of the sick who were brought to Him, or as when at Nazareth He could work no miracles at all; a limited knowledge, as when He had to ask for information, or when He owned that He did not know when the end of the world would be. Matthew and Luke are careful to remove from their portrait of Jesus any features that seem to derogate from His divine sonship, especially ignorance or powerlessness. Notice how Matthew transforms the answer given by Jesus, in Mark, to the young man who called Him "Good Master." In Mark He answers: "Why callest thou me good? there is none good but God alone." In Matthew He must not seem to repudiate His prerogative of divine goodness, and so He is made to answer: "Why doest thou ask me about goodness? There is but one who is good." Luke omits this episode altogether. But the human traits are not entirely obliterated in Matthew and Luke. Above all, the story of the temptation remains, and the entirely human episode of the agony in the garden. But in S. John, Jesus persistently thinks, speaks, and acts as one united to the Father; and therefore no human affection or weakness is ascribed to Him, neither the temptation in the desert, nor the moral struggle and uncertainty of Gethsemane, where, on the contrary, He goes forth, with full knowledge of what is coming, to meet His enemies and lays them low by the mere sound of His voice. Many of the divergences between the Evangelists are thus explained by this less or more accentuated tendency to exalt the divinity of Christ at the expense of His humanity.

But criticism is not satisfied with exploring the special character of each Gospel and of its discrepancy from the others. It has taken care to examine their resemblances and their mutual relations of origin and dependence. This had been done already for the Pentateuchal documents; but as applied to the Gospels the method has raised much more serious problems and yielded much more important results.

It had been long noticed, indeed it is evident at a glance, that the first three Gospels are strikingly alike—a fact which earns them their name of "synoptic." Above all they agree in their matter, of which one third is common to all three, and a considerable, though smaller, portion is common to two—Matthew and Luke. Considering the varied activity of Jesus and the range of His teaching this fact is surely significant.

But what is still more so is that the resemblance extends to the minutest particularity of the letter, not only in the discourses (which is strange enough, since Jesus spoke in Aramaic and not in Greek, and therefore the literal agreement of the translations would be most miraculous if a mere coincidence) but also in the narratives. And this is all the more marvellous that alongside of these exact resemblances there are found striking contradictions, and that what is common to all is mingled with what is peculiar to one. This phenomenon can evidently be explained only by the origin of the synoptics and their method of compilation. What then was this method? For over a century the problem has exercised the wits of the learned; but at last we can say that the synoptic question has received a unanimous and decisive solution in the hypothesis of a two-fold source. According to this hypothesis, the first source which explains the resemblance common to all three is S.

Mark, which has served as a basis for the other two. The chief reasons for this conclusion are the following: (1) With a very few exceptions all the material of Mark is found in the other two, while a great many parts found in Matthew and Luke are absent from Mark. If Mark was the common source of the other two, it is easy to understand how it might have been amplified by other sources, oral or written. But on the contrary it is hard to understand how an ampler source, like Matthew, could have been contracted into a smaller Gospel like Mark. We should have to say, with S. Augustine, that Mark wanted to make a compendium of the other two, or of one of them. But that is not possible, for on the one hand he leaves out facts of supreme importance, and on the other he dwells at greater length than they on matters of no doctrinal value. (2) The second reason is the order followed by the synoptics, sometimes the same, sometimes different. But Matthew and Luke never agree when they follow an order different from Mark; while Mark sometimes agrees with Matthew against Luke, sometimes with Luke against Matthew. This shows that Mark follows a common order from which one or other of his companions sometimes diverges. But even in so diverging they often show traces of their common source. For example, Matthew puts the cure of the leper after the Sermon on the Mount when Jesus was coming down with the crowd. But the word of Jesus, "See thou tell no man," supposes that the event was private, as it is represented in Mark. Luke represents the relatives of Jesus coming to Him after His sermon of parables held openly in the midst of the crowd. But the message brought to Jesus, "Thy mother and thy brethren stand *without*, and would see thee," supposes that the incident happened in a house just as Mark represents it to have happened. (3) What is true of the arrangement of the facts is equally true of their presentment. The synoptics differ frequently in explaining the circumstances accompanying the principal fact. But here again Mark usually agrees with one of the other two, while these never agree against Mark—if we except a few details, chiefly of language, whose explanation can only be found in the composition of the synoptics. (4) Lastly, the language of Mark abounds in Hebraisms, which disappear to some extent in Matthew and Luke. Now it is not possible that Mark should have wantonly adulterated the Greek of Matthew and Luke, while it is quite understandable that the other two should have tried to correct and purify the language of the source from which they drew.

A second source has been sought for the parts common only to Matthew and Luke and consisting mostly in discourses of our Lord. This time it was necessary to search outside the synoptics and to suppose a source common to the two Evangelists which no longer exists and which has conveniently been called the *Logia* (sayings)—a Greek word by which Papias, one of the oldest ecclesiastical writers, designated the contents of the original work of the Apostle Matthew. And this for two reasons: (1) First of all it was noticed that the character of priority, that is, the older, unamplified form of these sayings, was not always found in the same Evangelist, as would be the case if one served as source for the other, but sometimes in Matthew and sometimes in Luke. (2) Next, the two Evangelists arrange the sayings of Jesus, which they both record, independently of one another. Matthew prefers to weave these short sayings into long discourses. Luke keeps them separate as far as possible. Matthew tries to fit the discourses, thus composed, into the narrative of Mark and has no need therefore to prefix any sort of historical introduction. Luke, on the other hand, weaves all that he has over and above Mark, comprising what he has in common with Matthew, into two narratives, one longer than the other, and inserts them into the common narrative of Mark in the form of two long parentheses. And since, by this arrangement, he does not use the incidents of Mark as opportunities for the sayings of Jesus, he prefixes to each of these sayings an historical introduction to explain the occasion of its utterance. (3) Lastly, the supposition of a source distinct from the synoptics is confirmed by the fact that both Matthew and Luke repeat the same saying of Jesus twice over whenever that saying is also recorded by Mark. The most natural explanation of this is like that given for the "duplicates" of the Pentateuch, namely, each Evangelist depends on two sources—Mark and the *Logia*. Then remain the parts peculiar to Matthew alone and to Luke alone. No general principle as to their origin can well be established. Now and then they might seem to be extracts from the *Logia*. More often they depend on a special source, oral or written.

Closely connected with the synoptics is the book of the Acts of the Apostles, originally a continuation of the Third Gospel. It is not therefore surprising that we find here the same phenomenon as in the synoptics. Here, too, the letter presents many contradictions—contradictions between one part and another of the book itself, as when the conversion of S. Paul is related three distinct times and not once with the same circumstances, and when his call to the apostolate of the Gentiles is referred to three different epochs in his career; contradictions also with the Pauline Epistles, of which the most notable are those relating to the meeting of Paul and Barnabas with the Apostles at Jerusalem, recounted also in the Epistle to the Galatians.

But again all this comes from and is explained by the general tendency of the book, which is to prove the primitive unity of Christianity and its origin from Christ. Wherefore it first describes the formation of Jewish Christianity by the apostolate instituted by Christ, and then the derivation of Gentile Christianity, represented by Paul, from Jewish Christianity represented by Peter. This is effected, on the one hand, by giving Paul more than his due, as when he is credited with the first preaching of the Gospel to the Gentile world, including Rome, where the Jews are represented as having previously heard only some vague rumour of Christianity; whereas in the Acts themselves, not to speak of the Pauline Epistles, there are unmistakable indications that prior to S. Paul's arrival Christianity was already established in Rome even among the Jews. On the other hand, the historical personality of Paul suffers some diminution when from the moment of his conversion he is put in a relation of such strict dependence on Jewish Christianity, and especially on the Church in Jerusalem, even as regards his mission to the Gentiles. Naturally such a portrait is contrary to that given us in the Epistle to the Galatians, whose aim is to show the immediately divine origin and absolute independence of Paul's apostolate to the Gentiles.

The contradictions met with in the Acts raise a question as to the composition of the book and its possible origin from written sources. Most critics are inclined to believe in several written sources, and in particular to mark off what is called the "We" document because it narrates in the first person plural, implying that the narrator shared the adventures he recounts. This source is thought to be the notes of a travelling companion of S. Paul's—notes which the compiler of the Acts has used without altogether succeeding in harmonising them with the rest of his narrative, just because the tendency of that narrative was absent from the simple diary of S. Paul's travelling companion.

In the Fourth Gospel we move in a different plane from that of the synoptics. The form is different, but, for the most part, the matter is also different. Thus the field of Christ's ministry is not the same; while in the synoptics it is exclusively Galilee, save for one week before His Passion, in the Fourth Gospel it is principally Judæa and Jerusalem. The character of the book is not the same; for while of their very nature the synoptics are histories in which narratives hold the chief place, and discourses are more or less strictly incidental to the narratives, in John the discourses hold the first place and the narratives only serve to introduce the discourses, or else to express, or as it were to materialise, their teaching in the language of fact. And to this we must add the aim of the Fourth Gospel, not contrary to but higher than that of the others, which explains its particular differences and divergences from them.

But notwithstanding the great difference that separates the Fourth from the other Gospels, it cannot be denied that there are points of contact and that John must have known and to some extent worked upon the synoptics. This is plain not only in the few places where John agrees with the others or borrows some saying from them, but also where he openly diverges from them. For he often lets us see that he does so consciously, and even alludes (albeit tacitly) without any embarrassment to the different opinion of former writers, as when he affirms that the Baptist had not yet been cast into prison when Jesus began to preach and baptise—meaning apparently to correct the Second Gospel, which says the contrary. From many indications which we cannot retail here, it seems clear that John was acquainted with the Second and Third Gospels, though it is doubtful whether he knew the First.

From what has been said so far we are clear as to what must be considered the assured results of criticism concerning the origin and composition of the historical books of the New Testament. They are chiefly relative. First come the Gospel sources—the *Logia* and Mark, whether in its present or another form. Then the Gospels of Matthew and Luke compiled from these sources, with their natural sequel, the Acts of the Apostles, which has sources of its own. Last of all S. John, a unique and first-hand document.

But who are the authors of these several Scriptures? This for criticism is a secondary question. If the traditional opinion as to the authors agrees with the assured results of criticism as to the composition, mutual dependence, and character of the Gospels, so much the better; if not, it must be abandoned. But it may be objected that logically we should begin with the question of authorship and then go on to other questions. By no means. The question of the composition and nature of a book does not depend on the name of the author or compiler but on a direct examination of the book itself. On the other hand, the question of authorship is sometimes very complex and only admits of an indirect solution. So in the case of the Gospels. The tradition which ascribes them to those whose names they bear finds indirect expression for the first time in Justin Martyr about the middle of the second century. We cannot say directly what this assertion of Justin's is worth or how it stands in regard to all the generations between him and the origin of the Gospels. At most we can make more or less probable conjectures on the matter. Logic requires that we should begin by examining the books themselves which are before our eyes, and then pass on to examine this or that assertion as to their authorship. The latter investigation can be greatly aided by the former, but not *vice versa*.

This granted, there is no reason why the two sources of the Gospel should not be attributed, as they are by Papias, one to Matthew and the other to Mark; on the other hand, it is not very likely that the Third Gospel was written by Luke, the companion of S. Paul, since it is certainly by the author of the Acts; and the Book of Acts, which is at contradiction with itself and with the Pauline Epistles concerning many particulars about S. Paul, can hardly have been written by a close companion of his. All we can say is that one of the sources of the Acts is the work of a travelling companion of S. Paul, who was probably S. Luke; whence the whole work, of which the Third Gospel is part, came to be ascribed to the said Luke. Still less likely is it that the First Gospel was written by the Apostle Matthew if, as we have said, it was compiled from the Second Gospel (written in Greek) and by one who was not an eye-witness of the events recorded. Here, too, it is probable that the name of the author of one of the sources—the *Logia*—has been given to the whole work. Far more complex is the question of the authorship of the Fourth Gospel, nor can we here even touch upon it. Suffice it to say that the traditional opinion squares badly with the nature of the book as revealed by an internal examination and a comparison with the synoptics.

Of the other New Testament books we can speak but briefly. The Pauline Epistles for the most part are frankly admitted by criticism to be authentic, notwithstanding the hypercritical objections of the Dutch school. Exception however must be made not only of the Epistle to the Hebrews, which bears no writer's name, either in itself or in the most ancient tradition, but also of certain epistles professing to be by S. Paul, such as those to Titus and Timothy. Also the Catholic Epistles are generally considered pseudonymous. This conclusion is founded on a comparison of such Epistles with the undisputedly Pauline Epistles, and with the conditions, otherwise ascertained, of the time to which they are ascribed and with the qualification of the persons supposed to be their authors. The name of this or that apostle which stands at the beginning is, for criticism, no sufficient proof of their authorship. The publication of books under another's name was not so unusual or so discreditable in former times. Very little later than the New Testament we find, for example, the Revelation of Peter, the Gospel of Peter, the Preaching of Peter—all of which are pseudonymous. We find the like in Judaism about the time of Christ. Not only were apocalyptic writings ascribed to some great name of the past, such as Moses, Enoch, Isaiah, etc., but the sapiential literature, and especially the canonical Book of Wisdom, was credited to Solomon. Analogous examples occur in classical literature. Not to speak of others, a great mass of writings, evidently not genuine, has come down to us under the name of Pythagoras. This happens more easily in regard to letters, especially as the epistolary form is often itself a mere literary fiction. Pseudonymity is therefore not necessarily dishonest or immoral; it was one of the many recognised literary artifices of antiquity.

The criticism of the New Testament, like that of the Old Testament, involves many though still graver consequences for theology.

(1) First of all we find that it confirms that notion of inspiration forced upon us by the literary composition of the Pentateuch and of the other historical writings of the Old Testament. Those theologians who, as we have said, have given up the ancient and traditional notion of verbal inspiration were forced to do so by a comparison of the Gospels which made it impossible to believe that God had inspired the different Evangelists to report in a different form words (like those of the eucharistic institution) uttered but once by Christ and therefore only in one form. But even in such cases we find it is not a

question of merely verbal difference. The difference even of more or less, so common in the Gospels, is sometimes indeed a real difference; but often the very same saying of Christ is reported in a different sense in different Gospels, as is evident from the context or from some word changed or added. A still more decisive argument against the old mechanical idea of inspiration is found in the manner in which the Gospel sources are not only drawn upon by the successive Evangelists but modified as to their arrangement and argument. Had God formed the ideas and then transmitted them to the Evangelists, we should have to say that, being dissatisfied with His first attempt, He had repeatedly revised, corrected, and rearranged it like any human author.

Furthermore, the said mode of procedure on the part of the Evangelists shows that they did not consider their predecessors to be inspired in the old sense of the word, else they would have scrupulously respected their arrangement, their arguments, and even their very words. Plainly S. Luke in his prologue does not consider himself or his predecessors exempt from the need of labour nor immune from error. He implies that the composition of a Gospel supposes the possibility of ever new attempts, and is so high and hard an enterprise that no one Evangelist can hope to accomplish it perfectly.

(2) In the second place theology has to learn that

in the New as in the Old Testament there are, strictly speaking, no historical books but only sacred narratives shaped in great part by the faith in whose service they are written. The original sources are amplified by the successive writers and receive a new form and a new content; and this not because the later writers have made fresh investigations and acquired a more exact knowledge of the facts. Were it so they would agree and not differ among themselves more and more. Whence it is plain that the successive changes depend only on the peculiar religious tendencies of each writer.

But one may object that Luke declares at the outset that his intention is to write "accurately and in order." To which we answer that anyone who compares the Third Gospel with the Second will soon see what sort of "order" Luke has in mind. He puts the preaching at Nazareth at the beginning of Jesus' ministry; then the first day at Capernaum; and then the call of the first disciples. Mark, on the other hand, puts the preaching at Nazareth much later; begins with the call of the disciples, followed by the first day at Capernaum. The reason why Luke has changed the order of Mark is evidently not an historical one. For even he (v. 23) shows that he knew that the preaching at Capernaum came before that at Nazareth, and (v. 38) that the call of the disciples came before the day at Capernaum. But he prefers another order, because the preaching at Nazareth represents for him the preaching of Christianity among the Jews, and that at Capernaum its proclamation to the Gentiles; and because in the miraculous draught of fishes, connected with the call of the disciples, he sees a figure of the abundant results of the apostolic preaching which succeeded the preaching of Christ. The "order" of Luke is not determined by historical but by doctrinal and allegorical motives. And therefore the same can be said (or rather, after a comparison with the other synoptics, must be said) of that *acribia*, or accuracy, of which Luke makes profession in his prologue.

It may also be objected that Luke's object is to demonstrate the Christian faith: "*That thou mayest know the truth of those matters wherein thou hast been instructed.*" And so also S. John: "*These things are written that you may believe that Jesus is the Christ, the Son of God.*" And if so, the Gospel story should, of its very nature, be materially exact, else it could have no demonstrative value.

But first of all, be it noted, that the Gospels were not written to argue unbelievers into belief, but to illustrate and strengthen the faith of believers. If at times they mingle apologetic with doctrinal instruction, it is only indirectly and with a view to arming believers against the hostile controversy of the Jews. And this is clear not only from an inspection of the Gospels but from Luke's prologue, where he says that he is going to relate matters which (as the Greek has it) "have been fully established amongst us"; and this to Theophilus, who has already been briefly instructed in them and only needs a better knowledge of their certainty and security. No doubt, in order to support the faith of its readers, the Gospel story ought to be true and real and founded on the witness of "those who from the first have seen for themselves and have been ministers of the word of God." But as here the faith of the readers does not need to be wakened for the first time, since it is already alive and active both in reader and writer, it spontaneously rests upon and colours the narrative—transforming it, to some extent, so as to make it a more effectual expression of the object of faith. For this reason the Gospel story is at once the cause and the effect, the root and the blossom of faith. It is the result of two opposite tendencies—one toward the material truth of fact, the other toward a higher order of truth than that of historical exactitude. Wherefore the Gospel literature is a unique sort of literature determined by the peculiar double character of its object.

We find a parallel to the method followed by the Gospels in the allegorical interpretation so much in use among the ancient Hebrews, among the early

Christians, and in the Gospels themselves, according to which biblical texts and facts receive a higher sense conformable to the interpreters' own faith, but differing from and even irreconcilable with the literal sense. Here also it is faith that seeks a support and means of expression for itself. The Encyclical denies that it is possible to explain the facts that we have noted in the Gospels by means of old-world usages and by methods framed in the exigencies of the religious life. But the facts cannot be denied, and all we can do is to try and explain them.

From the nature, therefore, of the Gospels, as determined by criticism, it follows that we must distinguish two elements in them: one corresponding to historical reality, the other to the supernatural reality of faith. It is not true that we make a clean-cut division of the documents, assigning those to external history, and these to internal history—that is, to the history of faith. The two elements are for the most part so blended that they can be distinguished but not separated. It is certain, however, that faith-truth is not always historical truth, but often only historical fiction. And therefore since it is faith-truth that governs the Gospels from beginning to end we must not always expect to find historical truth as well. It is found in different measures in different Gospels, most of all in Mark, least of all in John.

Still more false is it that we allow to faith-truth

only a subjective existence in the mind of the believer—as the Encyclical seems to say. For us, the realities of history and of faith are equally objective but belong to different orders of truth—the former to the sensible and natural order, the latter to the super-sensible and supernatural. And for this reason they are the objects of two sorts of knowledge. Historical truth can be established by means of sensible experience; which experience, though a useful means, is not sufficient for the knowledge of faith which postulates a supernatural light. Else faith and historical knowledge would be the same thing—an identification replete with preposterous consequences. All this is so obvious that it is truly astonishing to see how the Encyclical repudiates it to the extent of denying that history being concerned, solely with phenomena, cannot as such prove the existence of God or His intervention in human affairs. But even profane history allows that its competence ceases with phenomena—with the facts and their interconnection. To investigate their inwardness and their ultimate causes belongs to a higher science called the philosophy of history.

When religious history is in question, to reason about the value which its facts possess in relation to God and the supernatural order has never hitherto been regarded as the business of the historian, whose only concern is to prove the existence of the facts, but as exclusively the business of the theologian who is occupied with the science of faith.

Now let us apply all this to the much-abused distinction between the Christ of history and the Christ of faith. In Himself Christ is one, but He can be considered as the object of history and the object of faith. As man, the person of Jesus and His outward words and actions were matters of sensible experience, and in this sense He belongs to history. As Christ (that is, as united to God in a quite unique manner and as a mediator of revelation and grace between us and God) He can only be apprehended by a divine and spiritual light; and in this aspect He belongs not to history but to faith. When Peter, pondering the words and deeds of Jesus, saw that He was the Christ, the Son of God, it was said to him: "Flesh and blood hath not revealed it to thee, but my Father who is in Heaven"; and in the Fourth Gospel this is extended to all believers. "No man cometh to me unless the Father who sent me draw him." What is revealed by flesh and blood is history; what is revealed by the Father is faith.

Another reason for distinguishing between the Christ of history and the Christ of faith is that there are two distinct states or stages in His life. First, that of His mortal life, in which He converses with men as men do with one another. Then that of His glorified life, beginning at His resurrection, in which

He still holds converse with us in a spiritual and invisible manner. In the first stage He acted simply as a prophet, preparing the Kingdom of God, stirring men up to repentance, and teaching them by word and example to live according to God's will. In the second, having risen to a new and spiritual life, He imparts to us His own spirit; that is, He lives His own life in us, not only in each of us singly but also in the Church collectively, thus leading us to share already, and in germ, the higher life of the world to come. In this life of Christ in us, manifested internally by the communication to us of His Holy Spirit, and externally by our fulfilment of His commandments, stands the whole essence of Christianity. Read the Epistles of S. Paul, throbbing with the full life of nascent Christianity, and say if there be aught else than this. Even the distinction between the Christ of history and the Christ of faith has already been made by S. Paul, albeit in other terms. He distinguishes between Christ, according to the flesh and according to the spirit. For example, consider carefully his definition of the Gospel at the beginning of the Epistle to the Romans: "The Gospel of God which He foretold by His prophets in the Holy Scriptures, concerning His Son, who, according to the flesh, was born of the seed of David, and according to the Holy Spirit was predestined to become the mighty Son of God by His resurrection from the dead." A different sort of existence demands a different faculty of apprehension; the mortal life of Christ, as evident to the senses, is an object of history; His spiritual life in the faith and in the Church can only be known—at least in its entirety and its inward nature—by means of the experiences of faith. But this second kind of life can also be at least *represented* under an historical form, and this gives rise not only to a distinction but to a separation between the historical Christ and the Christ of faith. The supernatural life of Christ in the Church has expressed itself outwardly in conformity with outer circumstances, and has thus gradually given birth to permanent ecclesiastical institutions. Now the Evangelists, in order better to signify the dependence of these institutions on the spirit of Christ, ever living in the Church, have thrown their origin back into the very history of the mortal life of Jesus. And in so doing they act with even more right than the authors of the Pentateuch, who refer all Jewish laws and institutions back to the days of Moses. And therefore criticism does well to distinguish what is history proper from what is merely an historical form of *representing* those supernatural facts which the Church's faith has brought forth.

Nor in making this distinction or separation does criticism (as some would pretend) rest on an *a priori* principle—on theories of "transfiguration" and "disfiguration," but, as ever, on the examination of texts and facts. Take for example the institution of the free and universal Church—independent, that is, of the bondage of the law and of the Jewish nationality. Such a Church came into existence very gradually after the resurrection of Christ. Had it been instituted directly by Jesus upon earth, or quite suddenly after His resurrection, it would be impossible to explain the conduct of the apostles who remained for a long time attached to the synagogue. Still more utterly inexplicable would be Paul's great struggle against the Jew Christians (in which, to say the least, he was not backed up by the other apostles) in the cause of the universality of Christianity and of its independence of Judaism. Yet it was Paul more than any other who helped to found the Catholic Church. But even the Evangelists tend, each in his own way and degree, to ascribe its foundation to the historical Christ. This tendency is but faint in Mark, much more pronounced in Luke, and most of all in Matthew, who puts the institution of the Church into the lips of the risen Christ, and makes the earthly Christ foretell the universality of an external institution of his own, analogous to the Jewish Church. But the process culminates in S. John, where Christianity is represented as being, already in the lifetime of Jesus, a religion of its own nature universal, a worship in spirit and in truth, perfectly distinct and separate from Judaism. In the Fourth Gospel we find already formally realised, and even surpassed, those results which were only obtained by S. Paul after a long and fierce struggle.

As the supernatural life of Christ in the faithful and in the Church has been clothed in an historical form which has given birth to what we might somewhat loosely call the Christ of legend, so the same life has been submitted to a doctrinal elaboration or explanation which has given birth to the Christ of theology or dogma. Christ imparts to us His Spirit, and therewith a divine life. What then are the bonds that unite Him to God? In what way does He so possess the Spirit as to be able to impart it to us? This is the fundamental problem from which all Christian theology has sprung. First an explanation was sought in the notion of the Jewish Messiah corrected by the facts of Christian history. The Messiah was not to be an earthly king, as the Jews imagined, but a heavenly king entering into His glory through suffering. And at His resurrection He received the Spirit, and so became "Christ according to the Spirit." This is the notion expressed by Peter, in the Acts of the Apostles, on the day of Pentecost, and that also inspires the narrative which is the basis of the synoptics, in which, however, Jesus receives the Spirit even before His resurrection:—in Mark, at His baptism, before the beginning of His ministry; in Matthew and Luke at His very conception, although the descent of the Spirit at His baptism is still retained. In the theology of S. Paul we already find a heavenly existence, anterior to His earthly existence, ascribed to Christ. From the foundation of the world He was "the heavenly Adam," "in the form of God," and in that sense the "Son of God"—a conception answering to that of the "Son of Man" in certain Jewish apocalypses. In the synoptics we also find the title, Son of God, attributed to Christ in this sense, and superimposed on the idea of His Messiahship. In the Fourth Gospel and the Epistle to the Hebrews we are carried a step further. The Son of God, pre-existing before His appearance on earth, comes to be identified with the Word of God, with Philo's "second God," with S. John's "God the only begotten," with the Epistle to the Hebrews' "radiance of His glory and express image of His substance." Therefore, in the Gospel of John, Christ is spirit by nature, and for this reason not only is no mention made of His conception by means of the Spirit, but the descent of the Spirit on Him at His baptism is considered merely as a sign to the Baptist that Jesus is He who baptises, not merely with water like John, but with the Spirit.

All these various successive and sometimes overlapping conceptions are evidently elaborated to explain that one fact of which Christian faith has continual and ever new experience, namely, that Christ lives in us and that it is He who baptises with the Holy Ghost. This fact supposes an intimate and unique communion with God, owing to which Jesus is able to impart God and God's spirit to us also—a communion so unparalleled as for ever to transcend our imagination and understanding, and for this reason never to be adequately expressed by even our sublimest theological explanations.

Hence it was that Christianity felt free in the early ages to give expression to its faith in the language of any speculative system current among the faithful for the time being. Its principal and even sole interest was in the realities experienced by faith. Explanations and theories had but a relative value in its eyes so far as they served better to communicate those realities and reproduce the same experiences in others. Look at S. Paul, for instance. Although he had a very complicated and artificial theology of his own, yet he protested that he desired to know nothing but Christ crucified; that is, to experience the life-giving efficacy of the death and resurrection of Christ. He did not scorn theology, but made use of it as an instrument of faith. He gives it a relative, but certainly not an absolute, value.

In the beginning therefore we find not strictly-defined doctrines or dogmas, but a faith that is "lived" intensely. Definitions began where speculation concerning the person of Christ "went too far" (2 John, ix.), in such sort as to make Him a purely ideal being and to destroy the historical Christ. Such definitions were rather negative than positive in their aim—which was to keep speculation within the due limits imposed by faith and history. It is thus against the Gnostics, who denied the reality of Christ's humanity, that the books of the New Testament, and especially the catholic and pastoral epistles, are chiefly directed. The Gnostic theology is styled a "science falsely so named"; its professors are called vain babblers, seducers, and otherwise laden with reproaches.

We are far from wishing to follow the lines and methods of Gnosticism. Not only have we no desire to overpass the due limits of theological speculation, but, while respecting it within its proper limits, we would give it at most a relative and not an absolute value. It is not from theological speculation of itself that we draw our spiritual life, but from Christ, whose personality and value theology may in some degree help us better to understand and express. By means of history we see in Him a man who has taught us by word and example; by means of faith we experience in Him the Saviour whose death and resurrection have given us a new life. So, with the eye of criticism, we discern in the Gospels the historical Christ; but not everywhere, for we know how to distinguish between the Christ of history and the Christ of legend and theology. With the eye of faith we see, whether under the Christ of history, or of theology and legend, that "Christ according to the Spirit," to the sole saving knowledge of whom the Evangelists have exclusively devoted their labours.

### (*c*) *Criticism and the Development of Christianity*

The critical method applied to the history of Christianity has yielded results no less decisive.

The traditional apologists have been wont to view the Church as an institution leading a life apart from the surrounding social and political world, growing and shaping itself according to peculiar laws of development, whose largely miraculous character forbids their verification. This ancient conception of the Church as the work of the *Logos*, and as a domain closed to the influence of those laws which govern the growth of human societies, having once obtained footing in the great historical construction of Eusebius, has for long ages been the postulate of all Catholic ecclesiastical history.

A prepossession of this kind, joined with the notion of revelation as being, before all, a communication of unchangeable abstract propositions, led to another assumption, namely, that the dogmatic affirmations, which gradually became part of the inherited intellectual explanation of faith, as well as the external forms progressively assumed by the ecclesiastical organisation, existed, at least implicitly, from the very beginning in the preaching of Jesus, in the faith of the first Christians, and in the teaching of the Fathers.

Historical criticism has purged our minds inexorably of these prepossessions. For criticism, Christianity is a fact like any other, subject to the same laws of development, permeated by the same political, juridical, and economic influences, liable to the same variations. Its quality of religious fact does not rob it of those other qualities which belong to every historical fact in which man's spiritual activity has found expression.

And therefore criticism, without any preoccupation, has studied the fact of Christianity in its historical context both as to its origin and its universal propagation. Studying and comparing the New Testament documents, considering the date of their composition and the practical scope of their several authors, it has, as we have seen, put it beyond doubt that their narrative shows traces of an elaboration of the person and teaching of Christ accomplished in the religious consciousness of the first two or three generations of believers. And then setting itself to discern, through these incrustations formed round them by an exalted faith, the authentic words of the Master and the simple theme of His discourses, it has been driven to the conclusion that the Gospel of Jesus was a persistent and enthusiastic proclamation of a coming kingdom of God; that it was free from all admixture of a materialistic eschatology; that at bottom it was an earnest and authoritative call to purity of heart. All the rest, that is, the wondrous affirmations as to the personal relations between Christ and the Father (so far as they exceed the then common identification of the Messiah with the Son of God), the ever more inward and spiritual conception of the Messianic kingdom, the special description of the Church or community of the faithful as the earthly equivalent of the heavenly kingdom—all this represents the formulation of new ideas evoked by Christian experience, especially in the more intellectual and cultivated followers of the Gospel, and notably in S. Paul. Such a criticism of the historical substance of Christ's teaching does away with the possibility of finding in it even the embryonic form of the Church's later theological teaching. So too an impartial study of the patristic tradition (preceded by a careful study of the authenticity of the documents to be used, and accompanied by a constant resolve not to read earlier witnesses in the light of later theological conceptions) has proved how idle it is to look there for the fundamental lines of Catholic theology as systematised by the scholastics and adopted in the definitions of Trent. What, without prepossession, must be admitted is, a progressive development of Catholic theology springing from the ineradicable need of supplying an intellectual embodiment and expression for that religious experience which, once evoked by the preaching of Christ, has remained substantially the same thing under all its successive embodiments.

An ancient legend told by Rufinus in the fourth century relates how "after the Lord's ascension the Apostles received orders to separate and spread over the world to preach the word of God. Before separating they took counsel and agreed on a common rule of belief lest they should be found teaching different doctrines. Full of the Holy Ghost they composed the creed."* Thus in the fourth century the belief had gained ground that the principal dogmas of Christianity had been formulated by the Apostles, fresh from the teaching of their Master and filled with the Holy Ghost. Modern criticism has not only shown this legend to be false but has striven to show, positively, that it is arbitrary and aprioristic to hold that the dogmas of faith go back,

* Rufinus, *Com. in Symb.*

in their present expression, to the primitive teaching of Christ and his immediate followers. Every day brings new successes in the endeavour to mark, by means of a critical analysis of documents, the slow, and at times imperceptible, evolution of Christian psychological experience toward the reflex formulation of dogma—an evolution guided by the necessity of finding theological formulas to foster and direct the original religion of the Gospel, which consists in the expectation of a kingdom of Heaven upon earth, in the felt solidarity of all souls in relation to their common good, and in trust and confidence in the Heavenly Father.

The Encyclical, it is true, upbraids our criticism with starting from the assumption "that everything in Church history is to be explained by 'vital emanation,' and that every event is the outcome of some want and should therefore be considered as historically later than that want."* Herein it seems to reproach us with an assertion whose contrary is simply historically unthinkable and theologically erroneous. As we have already said, the history of the Church as a living society is, in fact, governed by the same laws as other social institutions. Now it is an elementary law of life, in all its manifestations, that every organ answers to some vital need and that every output of energy is determined

* *Modernist History and Criticism*, Sec. 4.

by some deep exigency of the subject. Moreover, it seems to us as theologically incorrect to suppose that ecclesiastical history is a triumph of caprice and lawlessness, as it is thoroughly orthodox to believe in a divine Providence whose rule admits nothing superfluous, and which takes care that the course of events and the development of religious ideas in the Church are reached according to the varying but normal exigencies of the faithful. Nor are these mere aprioristic assumptions which vitiate the impartiality of historical research. History is within its province in seeking to determine the immanent reasons of facts and to trace the impalpable but very real exigencies whence the events recorded flow by logical necessity. History which fails to do this does not merit the name.

The conclusions of such a method, applied to the history of Catholicism, are simply disastrous to the old theological positions. Instead of finding from the first at least the germs of those dogmatic affirmations formulated by Church authority in the course of ages, we have found a sort of religion which was originally formless and undogmatic, and which came gradually to develop in the direction of definite forms of thought and ritual owing to the requirements of general intercourse and to the need of giving abstract expression to the principles which should shape the religious activity of the faithful. And this was effected partly by the efforts of Christian thinkers and partly by the negation of the positions adopted by heretics. The Gospel message could never have lived and spread abroad in its primitive spiritual simplicity. When it passed the borders of Palestine and was found to be of universal import, in order to evoke, in other peoples, the same religious experiences—unselfishness, inward purification, hope in a supernatural reward of righteousness, reliance on Jesus the Christ and Redeemer—it had to adapt itself to their mentality and to present Christ, with His message of redemption, in a different garb from that which He assumed in his Jewish surroundings and in the popular prophetic tradition.

Wonderfully flexible in its psychological simplicity, like every religious revival, primitive Christianity spread over the Roman world, that is, over the countries bordering the basin of the Mediterranean, adapting itself to the mentality and spiritual education of every region and borrowing from each the elements most suited for its own further development. This work of adaptation (accompanied by the spontaneous accommodation of the Gospel message to the ever more inexplicable delay of the Advent, whose nearness Christ had predicted) was completed in a relatively short time and, thanks to the influence of so great a religious thinker as S. Paul, has left its traces in the narratives of the life of Jesus which were primarily rather doctrinal and hortatory than strictly historical. Such elaborations affected most especially those doctrines that afterwards became fundamental for Catholicism—the Trinitarian and Christological dogmas, and the organisation of the Church.

This Church which lay beyond the horizon of Christ's outlook, bounded by the Parousia, grew up naturally among His followers and quickly passed from the charismatic hierarchy of his first days, arranged according to personal graces and gifts of the Spirit, to the official and monarchic hierarchy arranged according to measures of jurisdiction and sacramental power.

As to Trinitarian and Christological dogma, criticism has marked the various stages of its progress on its way to the lucid affirmations of the second Council of Nicea. The continual exultation of Christ in the esteem and affection of His followers, the various formulas invented to express his supernatural dignity according to the philosophical and theological language of the converted nations, combined with the sudden elaboration of certain Hebrew conceptions recast and catholicised by S. Paul, all evoked a rapid development of the intellectual elements latent in that spiritual movement set going by the Gospel message. The Acts (ii. 22), echoing the primitive Christian teaching, speak of Jesus as "A man to whom God has borne witness by miracles and wonders and signs wrought by His means." He is the Messiah upon whom an ignominious death has conferred heavenly glory, and who must soon return to inaugurate His kingdom. Such was the simple and deep faith of the first disciples. But Christ has called all the members of the human family to be sons of God, and has presented Himself as their archetype. He is, therefore, Himself pre-eminently the Son of God, according to the prophetic tradition which attributes that dignity to the Messiah.

Side by side with this profound elaboration of the simple Gospel ideas of Christ's personality there was a development of the idea of the Holy Spirit. As is usual at the beginning of any new religious upheaval, extraordinary phenomena, startling manifestations of a supernatural energy, took place in the little communities excited by the eager expectation of a universal renewal of all things. This energy or power, which took possession of the souls of men saturated with biblical lessons and narratives, was spontaneously identified with the Spirit of Javeh, to which the Old Testament usually ascribed any action that seemed to exceed the normal faculties of man. A natural relationship soon came to be established between the Father (to whom was directed the filial devotion of the faithful), the Son (who was the giver of the Spirit, that is, of power to become sons of

God) and the Spirit (who was the cause of the more striking manifestations of the new faith). And since it was especially at baptism that these surprising and mysterious effects of conversion were more manifestly displayed, it was in connection with this initiatory rite that Christians first formulated the invocation of the Trinity—a formula unknown to S. Paul. From baptism the Trinitarian formula passed, as Justin teaches us, into the liturgy.

Upon these elementary data, the still timid and hesitating expressions of the latent intellectual and dogmatic implications of Christian religious experience, there came to be based a vast theological structure whose beginnings and developments are not difficult to trace. S. Paul had already speculated as to the pre-existence of Christ, as to Christ's identity with the Holy Spirit, as to the effects of the said Spirit, which did not merely (like the Spirit of Javeh in the Old Testament) augment man's physical and natural energies, but transformed man's inner life, raising it to a higher level of existence and operation. And by such speculations he led the way in that sort of reflection which tends to express in precise philosophic categories the relations existing between those realities which feed and foster the Christian life.

The translation of the Hebrew conception of the Messiah into the Platonic idea of the *Logos* marks a culminating point in this theological elaboration.

Here the Messiah dreamt of by souls anxiously awaiting the redemption of Israel was identified with the abstract notion, essentially Hellenic, of a cosmic intermediary between the world and the Supreme Being. A Hebrew conception possessing certain moral and religious values, but otherwise unmeaning for the Hellenic mind, was translated into Alexandrine terminology in such a way as to retain those values in another and more metaphysical setting. To us to-day the lines pursued by this rapid evolution of ideas give the impression of a cold, aprioristic system. But in reality this progress of Christian life towards a better formulation of itself was the collective work of multitudes who "lived" their faith in thought as well as in word, action, and feeling.

Christology, so closely bound up with Trinitarian theology, naturally underwent in its turn a parallel and dependent development. The Messianic notion of the Son of David, and the apocalyptic notion of One who was to appear in the clouds, and the title "Son of God," which in Hebrew was synonymous with the Messiah, once transferred to Greek soil, where parentage between gods and heroes was a common belief, opened the road to the notion of a unique relation between Christ and the Father, and even of an identity of nature.

Finally, as regards the organisation of the Christian communities, they had come by the beginning of the second century to adopt the monarchic episcopate as the result of taking over certain offices and titles, partly from the synagogue, partly from the Hellenistic confraternities and societies.

The display of so vigorous a development, accomplished in the bosom of the communities at a time when the empire was doing its best to stifle the Gospel, is one of the most remarkable features of early Christian history. Not only was persecution unable to crush the nascent religion, it could not even arrest that healthy effort of the experience originated by Christ to evolve from itself a dogmatic formulation and an authoritative organisation by which to feed and foster the new Christian conscience, and to enable the Church to provide her ministers with a creed and an authority for the furtherance of her spiritual conquests. As soon as the last persecution had proved a lamentable fiasco, and the astute Constantine had perceived the wisdom of attaching his fortunes to those of Christianity by making it a state religion, the Church was all ready for that first impressive display of her material and moral force, which took place at Nicea, where the Trinitarian dogma and the consubstantiality of the Word with the Father were solemnly defined. Thus at Nicea were definitively laid the bases of that structure of orthodox thought raised up in succeeding centuries.

Theological conflicts recommenced, however, very soon, and this time the disputes were mainly Christological. Apart from the short-lived Macedonian controversy (settled at Constantinople) about the relation of the Holy Ghost to the other Divine Persons, the war was waged over the relation of the human and divine elements united in the person of Christ. It is remarkable to notice the jealous watchfulness of the Christian conscience, lest in this search for a formula to express a fact beyond the ordinary range of human comprehension any sacrifice should be made of the religious experience of Christ's immanence in the soul or of His redeeming efficacy. Nestorianism with its sharp distinction of two persons in Christ, human and divine, implicitly imperilled the infinite value of His acts and so was condemned by the Council of Ephesus. Eutyches went to the opposite extreme, insisting on unity of person to the prejudice of duality of nature, thus putting the imposing figure of the Redeemer outside the ranks of humanity, and so was condemned at Chalcedon. Thus has Catholic dogma threaded its way between the extremes of error, being the intellectual expression of the deepest needs of the Christian conscience, which seeks in Christ at once the man who has suffered for us and the God who has merited for us.

But the Church, pushed by historical events into

the office of guide and controller of the peoples of the West, so strangely intermixed after the barbaric invasion, soon felt a need of new methods of propaganda and government. The strife with Monothelism (the last disguised remnant of the Monophysite heresy) is only a secondary episode of Oriental character in comparison with the grave problem facing the Church in the midst of a Society reduced to intellectual chaos and looking to her not only for religious instruction but also for the rudiments of philosophical and scientific education. Henceforth the arena of intellectual conflict is not theology, properly so called, but philosophy, or rather, philosophical apologetic. In the Middle Ages, in a Society she had moulded with her own hands and inspired with her own spirit, the Church's most urgent task was to shape or to adopt a philosophy which might serve as a preparation for dogma, as an instrument of intellectual and even moral discipline in every department of life. And this is just why the Church, at the beginning of the mediæval philosophical controversies, turned with sympathy to the realistic logic—although rejecting the metaphysic—of Aristotle, finding therein the most effectual formulation of a mental attitude towards reality in harmony with the requirements of the absolutist conception of religion and those of a theocratic use of moral and political power. Modern criticism has sought, as yet without full success, to call up from the past the various attempts made before arriving at that blend of Aristotle and Christian dogma which characterises the golden age of scholasticism. The problem of "Universals," contained in a text of Porphyry, which has reached us through Boëthius, was the nucleus of philosophic inquiry. The first essays at a philosophical apologetic were made in the Carlovingian schools, but with a result contrary to the Church's desire. Scotius Erigena was a solitary thinker far too deeply saturated with a mystical individualism to be able to provide the society, sheltered under the wings of the Papacy and the Empire, with the impersonal and absolute formulas of a satisfactory metaphysic. But the attempt which failed once was renewed with that courage which is inspired by the needs of a new age. Yet how many failures were necessary before arriving at a harmonious synthesis! The nominalism of Roscelyn, the conceptualism of Abelard, the realism of Bernard, the intuitionism of the S. Victors represent so many currents that strove to prevail in a conflict of ideas which but reflected those real conflicts between papal and imperial power by which Society was torn asunder. Finally, coinciding in time with that great papal theocracy which was the fruit of centuries of political effort, came the imposing construction of scholasticism, in which philosophy and dogma seemed to be harmonised, and whose mission it was apparently to bind intelligences in the bonds of a metaphysic which was in reality the most potent instrument of moral domination that the age of Innocent III. could have possibly desired.

It is in the fact that scholasticism was begotten by the practical needs of that age—that is, by the need of providing a philosophic and religious synthesis which should tie down man's spirit in a posture of humble submission in matters of reason and conduct—it is in this fact that criticism finds the chief reason of the slight historical consciousness of which scholasticism gives evidence. All the patristic sources, all the expressions of Christian experience fashioned by previous generations, are noticed and used by the scholastic divines only so far as they serve to support their intellectual positions. Nowhere do we find signs of an impartial inquiry as to what the primitive Christian fact was in reality; nowhere a docile acceptance of the genuine data of patristic tradition whenever these were opposed to their Aristotelian prepossessions. Scholasticism is precisely the intellectual expression of the Christian experience as adapted to the spiritual needs of the early Middle Ages. And this is why the Papacy has clung to it with a tenacity worthy of a better cause, and brought about its canonisation at the Council of Trent. It recognises instinctively (though not avowedly) in scholasticism the most effectual defence of that age in which its own authority reached a fulness of splendour soon afterwards lost irreparably. Even to-day it would fain rehabilitate scholasticism. But how is it possible to revive such a mode of apologetic now that criticism has, without any sort of prepossessions, reconstructed the whole story of the evolution of Christianity with all its successive stages and varieties of expression? Criticism has made us see how Catholic dogma has sprung entirely from the need of setting experience in harmony with the mind of the age, and the unchanging spirit of religion with the ever-varying expressions of thought. How can we refuse to accept these conclusions which are not the result of hair-brained speculation but of a most painstaking analysis of Christian documents? If the Church needed to oppose them uncritically with the assumptions of the Middle Ages, she would have to face disaster and bankruptcy. But there is no such need. Providentially the Church has not yet defined the relations between her immutability and her flexibility. And, therefore, we who believe in the harmony of faith and science, and who therefore accept the results of criticism as well as that measure of immutability required by the inherent truth of Christianity, have had recourse to certain new apologetic considerations which seem to us to possess an abundant persuasiveness in the eyes of our contemporaries. We have been able to show how spontaneous the evolution of Christianity has been, and yet how indispensable it has seemed at every historical crisis for the preservation of Christian piety, and how, without it, religion would have been perverted, weakened, and perhaps destroyed. Whence it follows that we cannot possibly deny the evolution of Catholicism.

As we cannot refuse the results (ever more or less imperfect) of social evolution, so, too, the whole process of Christian development, wrought by the Christian consciousness upon the religious experience of the Gospel, strikes us as something legitimate in itself which we are not free to accept or refuse, since in refusing it we should dry up the deepest roots of our spiritual life. And even if certain modes of thought, and certain conceptions of authority, transmitted to the Church from the Middle Ages, seem to us to have now grown to be encumbrances, we do not believe that we have, as individuals, any right to oppose them, but only to spread abroad among the masses of the faithful a consciousness of their inutility and obstructiveness. For a higher experience and expression of Catholicism must be the fruits of a more enlightened, more cultivated, more spiritual collective conscience. It is from this point of view that a conciliation of the rights of criticism with the deepest needs of faith seems possible to us. Everything in the history of Christianity has changed—doctrine, hierarchy, worship; but all these changes have been providential means for the preservation of the Gospel-spirit, which has remained unchanged through the ages. Of course the scholastics and the Fathers at Trent came into a much richer theological heritage than the Christians of the first century; but the religious experience, that in virtue of which they were Christians, was the same for them all. And for us to-day it is likewise the same, although it moves but slowly towards a new self-formulation, owing to the sway, no longer intellectual but simply juridical, of scholasticism, which has won the surely anomalous position of an "official" philosophy. The formulations of the past and of the future have been, and will be, equally legitimate, provided they faithfully respect the growing needs of evangelical piety, ever eager to find in reflex thought a better instrument for its own preservation and utterance.

Reasoning thus, we find ourselves undoubtedly in harmony with one of the fundamental tendencies of contemporary philosophy, and which is even considered the very condition of the possibility of a philosophy—the immanental tendency. According to this principle, nothing can enter into and get hold of man's spirit that does not spring from it and in some way correspond to its need of self-expansion. For it there is no fixed truth, no unalterable precept, that is not in some way self-imposed and innate. Applied to the history of Christianity this immanental principal provides the best defence for those positions which the Church has arrived at in obedience to the constant instigation of the collective conscience.

But this our agreement with the philosophy of immanentism has not preceded, but rather followed upon, the effort of scientific criticism to discern the objective evolution of Christianity through the darkness of the past. And here we must go on to discuss the philosophical charges which the Encyclical puts down to our account. Are they accurate? And where they are partly exact are they, as the Encyclical contends, anti-Catholic?

## SEC. 2.—THE APOLOGETIC OF THE MODERNISTS

### (*a*) *Are we Agnostics?*

Discussing the philosophy of the Modernists, the Encyclical reprehends its agnostic principles, its immanental method, its agnostic application to history of the postulates of the "transfiguration" and "disfiguration" of phenomena.

Let us speak, first of all, of our supposed agnosticism. It is based on the idea, says the Encyclical, "that human reason is wholly confined to the region of phenomena, that is, to what appears, and to the manner of its appearance. Beyond that it has no right, no natural power, to go." We hope to make clear the contradiction into which the Encyclical falls in its desire to prove us agnostics. Indeed, in the very same paragraph it credits us with opinions flatly incompatible with agnosticism. For it says that "they" [the Modernists] "have settled and determined that science and history must be atheistical;" and a little later it adds that, according to Modernists, "religion, whether natural or supernatural, must, like every other fact, admit of an explanation." With what consistency can the Encyclical reproach us in the same breath with an agnostic prepossession which forbids any affirmations of reason about the super-phenomenal, and also with an atheistic postulate in science and history, and with the principle that the origin and nature of religion admit of an explanation?

But let us overlook these little slips which the compiler of the document has made in the embarrassing task of squeezing Modernism into the antiquated categories of his own philosophy, and let us examine seriously if there be aught of agnosticism in our system. And let us begin from the definition of agnosticism formulated by its great leader, Herbert Spencer. His conclusion, expounded and defended in *First Principles*, is as follows: "If we look into the nature and value of religion and science we find in the former certain primary ideas and universally present elements, and in the latter certain truths not deducible from other truths, and therefore inexplicable. So that at the basis both of religion and science we come on a sort of neutral ground which evades our mental analyses—on a bundle of ideas and sentiments which we cannot account for. On this ground, faith and science may and should be reconciled. We should acknowledge this domain of the 'Unknowable'; but as being such we should carefully refrain from every sort of irreverent desire to penetrate its nature or to determine its attributes and modes of action by our puny metaphysical speculations."

Now this agnostic confession of impotence in the face of the mystery of the universe is radically opposed to our mind. Our apologetic is precisely an attempt to escape from this agnostic knowledge-theory by rising above it; just as agnosticism stands for an attempt to rise above materialistic positivism. The agnostic, saturated with rationalistic principles, can imagine no other forms of knowledge than the sense-experience of phenomena and the dialectical reason invoked to dissipate the formal arguments of religious philosophy in defence of certain theories about the origin of the universe and its dependence on a Supreme Being. As Kant had revealed the antinomies of the cosmological, the psychological, and the theological ideas, so Spencer, by means of pure argument, has tried to point out the arbitrary and aprioristic elements that enter into all our metaphysical and religious explanations of the real; concluding that there is a basis of reality impervious to our cognitive faculties, and on which we must not trespass.

Our own attitude with regard to knowledge and its value is radically different, and not only coincides with that more generally assumed by the philosophy of to-day, but is also in continuity with the general results of the criticism of science.

First of all we distinguish different orders of knowledge—phenomenal, scientific, philosophic, religious. Phenomenal knowledge embraces all sense-objects in their particularity; scientific knowledge applies its calculations to the various groupings of perceived phenomena, and gives expression to the constant laws of their changes; philosophical knowledge is the interpretation of the universe according to certain inborn categories of the human mind, and having regard to the deep-seated, unchanging demands of life and action; religious knowledge, in fine, is our actual experience of the divine which works in ourselves and in the whole world.

Naturally this does away with the old definitions,

inherited by scholasticism from certain classical sources, by which science was conceived as "the knowledge of an object according to its causes — efficient, final, material, and formal," and philosophy as "the knowledge of things human and divine in their ultimate causes." But it is not our fault that the philosophy of science has, on its part, demonstrated how much pure convention there is in every science; or if psychological analysis, in its turn, has shown the subjective and personal elements which contribute to the formation of abstract knowledge. So that to-day it is no longer possible to speak of a cognitive faculty which functions in complete independence of our subjective needs and interests, and arrives at a certainty and a truth which is "an equation of thought to thing" (*adaequatio rei et intellectus*). To-day speculation is recognised to be a sort of *action*, in the more general sense of the term, and to be subservient to action. The act of knowledge is the result of a laborious effort of the spirit to dominate reality and turn it to its own service by aid of certain mental *schemata*, or plans, in which it represents the useful relations and connections of objects.

Such a conception is liberating in the broadest sense. Considering the cognitive faculty as a function of man's whole inward life; always remembering the relation of strict solidarity between abstract thought and action; breaking down the fictitious barriers raised between thought and will by scholastic psychology, we contrive to give an enormous expansion to the region of "the knowable," and to show that man is able, although by forms of knowledge hitherto little appreciated, to attain to those higher realities, the intimate apprehension of which augments the value of life and enriches it with new possibilities. Just as science, by its combination of experiment with the laws of the calculus, extends our dominion over the physical world, and as metaphysics corresponds to the necessity of guiding our action by a fixed conception of the universe, so the needs of our moral life, and that experience of the divine which we possess in the hidden depths of our consciousness, issue in a special sense of spiritual realities which dominates the whole of our ethical existence.

For us it matters little to attain to God through the demonstrations of mediæval metaphysics or through arguments from miracles and prophecies, which offend rather than impress the modern mind, and evade the control of experience. We recognise in ourselves other powers of divine knowledge; we find in ourselves that inferential sense, of which Newman speaks, by which we can be assured of the presence of higher and ineffably mysterious powers with which we are in direct contact. Compared with this knowledge-theory of ours, agnosticism seems, as in fact it is, a cold, rationalistic system. We accept that criticism of pure reason which Kant and Spencer have made; but far from falling back, like Kant, on the aprioristic witness of the practical reason, or from ending, like Spencer, in the affirmation of an "Unknowable," we maintain the existence of other powers in the human spirit, every bit as reliable as the argumentative reason, for attaining to truth. It cannot be denied that our postulates are inspired by the principles of immanentism, for they all assume that the subject is not purely passive in its processes of knowledge and in its religious experiences, but brings forth from its own spiritual nature both the witness to a higher reality intuitively perceived and the abstract formulation of the same.

But is this principle of vital immanence so dangerous as the Encyclical seems to believe?

### (*b*) *Our Immanentism*

"Since—according to the Modernists—religion is nothing but a form of life, its explanation is to be found precisely in the life of man. Hence their principle of religious immanence. Furthermore, the first movement of every vital phenomenon, such as religion is said to be, is always to be ascribed to a certain need or impulse; speaking, then, more especially of the life of religion, its beginnings are to be ascribed to a certain sentiment or stirring of the heart." Even allowing for the unavoidable travesty to which our thought is subjected, owing to the attempt to express it in the categories of scholasticism, we recognise that these are, in substance, our ideas upon the origin of religion. Religion is shown to be the spontaneous result of irrepressible needs of man's spirit, which find satisfaction in the inward and emotional experience of the presence of God within us. In maintaining this are we in conflict with tradition? Let us see.

We must recognise, first of all, that the arguments for the existence of God, drawn by scholastic metaphysic from change and movement, from the finite and contingent nature of things, from the degrees of perfection, and from the design and purpose of the world, have lost all value nowadays. The conceptions on which these arguments rest have now, owing to the post-Kantian criticism both of abstract and empirical sciences and of philosophical language, lost that character of absoluteness which they possessed for the mediæval Aristotelians. Since the mere conventionality of every abstract representation of reality has been demonstrated, it is clear not only that such arguments fall to pieces but that it is idle to construct others of the same class. Hence it was natural to have recourse to the testimony of conscience in order to demonstrate the existence of God, or rather, to justify our faith in the divine. Thus an appeal was made to man's moral impulses, which, for the rest, are the most authorised witnesses in this matter, since the origin of religion is a fact of conscience and should be investigated accordingly. Such a mode of procedure is not only fully justified in itself, but has been held legitimate by the most illustrious representatives of Catholic teaching.

The judgment, "God exists," is, like every other judgment, either analytic or synthetic, or, to speak not with Kant but with the scholastics, is either necessary or contingent. But an affirmation of existence cannot be an analytical judgment; that is the notion expressed by the predicate ("exists") cannot, of itself, form part of the notion expressed by the subject. It must, therefore, be a synthetic judgment; and since Catholic philosophy does not admit judgments called synthetic *a priori*, we must conclude that it is synthetic *a posteriori*, that is, a judgment to be proved by experience and not by mere reflection. And since, in this case, there can plainly be no question of laboratory experiments, we must conclude that God's existence can be proved only by conscience and in the experiences of conscience. We are therefore perfectly logical in seeking to ground our affirmation of a transcendent divinity on the immanent needs of man's conscience, and in striving to follow up the deep aspirations and ever-recurring necessities which spur the will to raise itself with all its might towards God, who, as S. Augustine says, already works in us creating this desire to seek Him. So reasoning we are in perfect harmony with the scholastic as well as with the patristic tradition. The latter, more especially considering Aristotelianism fatal to the profession of Christian orthodoxy,* considered faith quite sufficient for itself and independent of philosophy. The former, although characterised by the predominance of realistic logic over mystical intuition, never forgot the moral argument when it wanted to prove the existence, the value, the purpose of spiritual realities. A few examples will show this.

Clement of Alexandria, in the *Stromata*, shows at length that the origin of things cannot be found by demonstration, but only by the spontaneous faith of the spirit which, instead of seeking God in the abstract principles of reason, should strive to acquire that self-discipline and strength which spring from the practice of the great virtues—charity, penitence, etc. Faith, he adds, is as needful for man as breath-

* "That miserable Aristotle who teaches the heretics a subtle dialectic which can say and unsay,—shifting in its conclusions, harsh in its arguments, fruitful of barren wranglings, a nuisance even to itself, ever retracting just because it treats nothing thoroughly." *De Praescr.*, vii.

ing is for life. Without faith no knowledge of the divine is possible. God is the object not of science but of faith. And man's spirit is pervaded by a divine and mysterious effluence (L. ii.).

Far more explicit are the declarations of Tertullian, who invokes in favour of Christianity, not philosophical systems and abstract theories, but the spontaneous testimony of the human soul: "Stand out before me, O Soul. If, as so many philosophers say, thou art a thing eternal and divine thou surely wilt not lie. If thou art a thing human and mortal, still less wilt thou lie in favour of a God who is no part of thee. I do not appeal to thee as trained in the schools, brought up among books, stuffed with academic learning. I call upon thee as simple and rude, as ignorant and uncultured, even as thou art possessed by those whose sole riches thou art. For I need thy very deficiencies." And it is from this unsophisticated soul, as it reveals itself prior to all instruction and cultivation, that Tertullian demands a spontaneous and unforced testimony in favour of Christianity. From its natural language, from its most ordinary movements, from its commonest aspirations, this great apologist draws a triumphant argument for the *humanity*, and therefore for the truth, of the Gospel message.*

Origen says that "the rational soul as it re-

* *De Tert. An.*, c. i., *et passim.*

cognises its own nature comes to withdraw itself from those objects which at first it had accounted gods; it conceives a natural love of its Creator, and following up this love, it takes for its Master Him who first revealed this doctrine to men and who to that end made use of disciples whom He had duly fitted for the work." *

But the Father who has most persistently appealed to the direct witness of the Spirit in favour of man's inward experience of the divine is S. Augustine. His saying, "Thou hast made us for Thyself and our heart is restless till it rest in Thee," is well known. His *Confessions*—that wonderful epopea of the transformation of a soul under the inward stimulus of the divine—abound with phrases alluding to that demonstration of God which every man can draw from the personal experiences of his own interior life. He speaks of the "wondrous and secret ways" by which God makes the soul aware of Him (v. 6, 7, 13), and he gathers up his own experiences in this wise: "Thou, O Lord, by a mysterious instinct, dost lead men unawares to hear and to perceive that which pertains to their uplifting" (vii. 6.)

Last of all, S. Thomas himself, though drawn to metaphysical speculations and full of trust in argumentative reasoning, allows due demonstrative value

* *Contra Celsum*, iii., 40.

to the living aspirations of conscience and to the deeper needs of the spirit. He constantly affirms that "a natural desire can never be a delusion" (I. q. lxxv. a. 6; C.G. ii. 55; iii. 51). Even the genuine scholastic tradition, far from holding that the moral argument is worthless or leads to subjectivism, uses it in its nicer demonstrations, such as those of the freedom of the will and the immortality of the soul. In fact it rests these two theses, so fundamental for Christian spirituality, solely on the argument from the testimony of conscience.

Thus we can maintain that our position as regards the proof of God is perfectly coherent with the best Christian tradition. Led as we are by the theory of sciences to a revision of all our empirical notions; enlightened as we have been by descriptive psychology as to the origin and value of abstract ideas in a way diametrically opposite to the scholastic theory of the *intellectus agens* and the *intellectus possibilis;* persuaded henceforth beyond doubt as to the natural conventions that enter into all our metaphysical conceptions of the real, we can no longer accept a demonstration of God supported by those "idols of the tribe"—the Aristotelian conceptions of motion, of causality, of contingency, of finality. We believe, moreover, it is better for the Christian conscience to allow explicitly that if the demonstration of God is essentially bound up with these conceptions then indeed criticism has definitively paved the way to atheism, but at the same time to affirm with the fullest conviction that there is another method of demonstrating that truth, the chief argument of all—older than scholasticism—the argument of the living and acting spirit which, amid all the contingencies of its surface life, bears in itself a restless hunger for the divine, and comes to live a more noble life only on condition of recognising this hunger and satisfying it with the religious experience that its surroundings and historical setting naturally impose upon it.

### (*c*) *Characteristics and Consequences of our Immanentism*

We are therefore immanentists. But immanentism is not that terrible evil which the Encyclical seems to suppose, but is the method followed by the best Christian tradition in quest of the divine. We must insist on this point to defend ourselves against certain undeserved rebukes administered to us by the Encyclical.

(1) First of all it tries to show an imaginary contradiction between our views and certain definitions of the Vatican Council which say: "If any assert that the one and true God, our Creator and Lord, cannot be known with certainty by the light of man's natural reason, arguing from things created,

let him be anathema." And again: "If any assert that divine revelation cannot be made credible by external signs, and that therefore men should not be moved to believe, except by inward experience and private inspiration, let him be anathema."*

Premising that the guiding Providence which shapes the Church's history takes care that the doctrinal formulas, devised at a particular crisis to meet the passing religious needs of the community at that time, are expressed with sufficient latitude not to be an obstacle to later requirements of the spirit, we reply that our views are quite reconcilable with the Vatican definitions.

As regards the first definition, it is easy to see that our contemporary idea of "the natural light of reason" is quite different from that of scholasticism. It is impossible for us of to-day to conceive a purely intellectual and speculative faculty, immune from all influence of the will and the emotions. To the latest psychology, reason seems more and more to be a sort of instrument of formulation and definition which human nature has instinctively fashioned for itself, and which it uses unconsciously in order to arrange, express, and control the experiences of the more elementary and universal faculties of will and feeling and external sensation.

The human subject is viewed now as a complexus

---

* *De Rev.*, i. and *De Fid.*, iii.

of energies of which each tends to the fullest possible self-expression in the daily expansion of life. For us reason does not exist as something abstract and apart. It exists only as a function of the instinctive faculties whose wants and successes it registers and classifies for future use. Undoubtedly the Thomistic theologians who formulated the above definition at the Vatican Council meant to say that the knowledge of God is attainable by the pure understanding working on our sense-impressions of the universe and arguing thence, syllogistically, to the existence of a first cause. But this does not hinder a mind, forced into agreement with the indisputable results of contemporary thought from declining to accept the definition in its scholastic sense, and taking it to mean that from the knowledge of itself and its own inward experiences (which are created things) the human spirit in its entirety (including reason, will, and feeling), can naturally arrive at a living certainty of the existence of God. And amongst these means of knowledge, taken in the widest sense, we must also set that quite indefinable experience of a divine impulse which reaches us, as members of a social organism, through past ages of collective religious life, and of an aspiration towards that fuller sense of a transcendent divinity which will be realised by the religious generations of the future.

As for the second Vatican definition, we fail to

see where we are in conflict with it. In the first place, it does not speak of faith in God but of revelation; that is, of a positive fact which we have already tried to explain in accordance with a critical study of those documents in which, as the Church teaches us, revelation is contained. That this revelation can only be transmitted by external signs is beyond question. But this does not alter the fact that our adhesion to those supernatural realities, which are the theme and argument of the said revelation is a result of internal experience. In this connection S. Thomas writes: "The teacher is not the cause either of the intellectual light or of the intellectual representations in the mind of the learner. But by means of his instruction he stimulates the learner to form within himself, and by the energy of his own intelligence, those conceptions whose verbal symbols have been presented to him by the teacher."* We can apply this illuminating reflection to the words of the Council. Sacred tradition communicates to us those external signs in which revelation has been recorded. The human mind ought not to remain passively receptive and inert in regard to them, because the religious experience, which they are designed to evoke, proceeds from the needs and interests of the spirit, and from the synchronous vibration of our whole moral being

*S. T., p. i. q. 117, a. 1.

with the divine word which is revealed, or reveals itself, through these outward symbols.

(2) None the less, the Encyclical accuses us of "scientific and historical atheism," *i. e.*, of holding that science and history should ignore the existence of God. How little this tallies with the charge of pseudo-mysticism is self-evident. Furthermore, it is an open absurdity, as we shall now show.

That only phenomena come within the jurisdiction of science and history is not our discovery, but the admission of all scientists and historians worthy the name who follow those methods and canons which scientific research now considers definitively established. Science and history aim at ascertaining facts and at indicating, as far as possible, the constant relations which obtain between the phenomena verified in the various fields of observation. But in making use, in their research, of the instruments at their disposal—experience, or artificial experiment in physics; documentary analysis in history—they are, or they ought to be, free from any sort of apologetic preoccupation. This science (of which history is now but a branch) is neither theist nor atheist; it is if worthy of the name, simply science. It is not we who have made it what it is. We have only accepted it and made use of it as being an impartial investigation of facts, and of facts only. Hence the reproaches of the Encyclical are somewhat astonishing. Is it not a received theological axiom that faith and science, as two rays from the same divine light, cannot contradict one another? This surely does not mean that faith is in harmony merely with a science expurgated *ad usum Delphini.* That would be an insult to the divine veracity. And therefore, being perfectly certain of an ultimate accord of faith and science, we should adopt, so to say, the most scientific science, that, namely, which is freest from all apologetic bias. And so we are not atheists in science but lovers of that true science which is indifferent to all those ultra-phenomenal problems, whose solution concerns the other faculties of man's spirit.

And when in fact we go beyond the territory of pure science, impelled by our need of faith in the divine, we see how the results of our scientific research are quickened by a new spirit and acquire far more precious and significant values. We see then in the world of physical phenomena a progressive expression of goodness, and we draw thence a firm faith in a higher principle, to which we cleave as to a Father who arranges providentially for the triumphant survival of the most serviceable elements of general existence. And in the world of history we see an all-present Will whose secret influence directs the moral progress of mankind. Thereupon the negative results of our criticism vanish before the strong affirmations of religious intuition. Criticism has destroyed the belief in the formal transmission of a primitive revelation. But beyond criticism there is a faculty which sees "in the Jewish religion a principle of life which may justly be called superhuman, and which, notwithstanding the limitations of knowledge, the seeming illusions of hope, the resistances of rationalism, of ritualistic customs, of theological inflexibility, tends to an ever more perfect self-expansion—a principle frail in appearance but formidable in reality. It is in truth that little stone which, striking against the base of the colossal statue of earthly empires and religions, has reduced them to dust, and has, in its own turn, grown to that great mountain upon which the whole human race can find standing-room."* Faith sees a continuous revelation from the Old to the New Testament by which the divine manifests itself more and more unmistakably. It matters little to faith whether or no criticism can prove the virgin-birth of Christ, His more striking miracles, or even His resurrection; whether or no it sanctions the attribution to Christ of certain dogmas or of the direct institution of the Church. As ultra-phenomenal, these former facts evade the grasp of experimental and historical criticism, while of the latter it finds, as a fact, no proof. But both these and those possess a reality for faith

* Loisy, *La Religion d'Israel*, p. 88.

superior to that of physical and historical facts. Without them, without such an expression of ultimate moral values, Christian religious experience would have lacked one of its most solid supports. In the entire psychological elaboration to which the faith of centuries has submitted the simple elements of the Gospel, faith sees no ordinary or natural effect, but one dependent on the assistance of that Divine Spirit which has fostered the life of Christianity from the beginning. The dogmas shaped by the abstract formulation of Christian experience, the Church organised by the needs of the community of the faithful, the sacraments sprung from the need of attaching to external symbols the remembrance of the work of redemption, and of sharing its immortal fruits by means suited to man's double nature of sense and spirit—all these seem to us indispensable for the uniting together of souls in one and the same religious life.

We unite ourselves to all the faithful in the same creed and the same ceremonies, knowing that these bind us by historical continuity with the work of Christ, and are the means by which the adherents of Catholicism are bound together in one and the same collective moral experience. And even if we could turn back to a simpler and more direct experience of Christianity, and could dispense with much that has been transmitted to us, yet our Catholic sentiment would forbid us to break with ancient and universal customs, even while prudently disseminating our simplification of the experience for which they stand.

This way of conceiving the legitimacy of the development of Christianity is rebuked by the Encyclical as subjectivism and symbolism. But subjectivism and symbolism can no longer be reproaches. The latest criticism of the various knowledge-theories points to everything in the realm of knowledge—the laws of science and the theories of metaphysics—as being subjective and symbolic. But this does not hinder every such creation of the human spirit in the various departments of its activity from having an absolute value. Also the world constructed by faith has its life-giving value, and is therefore something absolute in its own kind. As for symbolism, a symbol no longer means a fictitious, and perhaps fraudulent, substitution connected with ignorant or erroneous beliefs. It too is a reality of its own peculiar kind whereon faith confers an inestimable value by which it becomes the real vehicle and beneficent occasion of an uplifting of the spirit and of a deeper religious insight. And since our own life is—for each one of us—something absolute, nay, the only absolute of our direct experience, all that proceeds from it and returns to it, all that feeds it and expands it more fruitfully, has, in like manner, the value of something absolute. The point of the Encyclical's reproach is therefore blunted in these days.

### (*d*) *Transfiguration and Disfiguration*

With these terms the Encyclical designates the consequences which Modernists, as it conceives them, ought to draw from the application of their so-called agnosticism to history.

"The Unknowable they speak of does not present itself to faith as something solitary and isolated, but, on the contrary, in close conjunction with some other phenomenon which, though it belongs to the realms of science and history, yet to some extent exceeds their limits. Thereupon faith, attracted by the 'Unknowable' concealed under the phenomenal, takes entire possession of the phenomenon itself, and permeates it to some extent with its own life. Hence two consequences. First, a sort of 'transfiguration' of the phenomenon by what we may describe as an elevation above its proper conditions which renders it apt material for the divine form which faith is to bestow upon it. Secondly, a certain 'disfiguration,' as it may be called, of the same phenomenon, arising from the fact that faith attributes to it, when stripped of the circumstances of place and time, characteristics which it really does not possess."

Let us pass over agnosticism, of which we have already spoken, and the "Unknowable," of which no Modernist speaks, and let us come to that constant and ever-increasing alteration of historical reality which Modernists are said by the Encyclical to ascribe to the influence of faith. The reproach seems to rest on an equivocation. This alteration of the object, due to the faith which invests it, is either confined to the order of our knowledge, in which case it is simply undeniable; or it extends to the order of ontological reality, in which case we deny it as vehemently as does the Encyclical, which commits an unpardonable equivocation in not distinguishing between these two orders. Let us explain.

It is undeniable that an historical fact assumes ever larger proportions and ever deeper significance in the accounts of it transmitted from generation to generation of individuals interested in its ethical and religious values. Just because the practical consequences and the countless applications of that fact to man's moral life cannot at once be drawn out and illustrated, it needs a long time before men can clearly penetrate its whole vital significance. But this does not mean that the deeper and later experiences of its significance are something ontologically new or were not already contained potentially in the fact itself.

We allow that in relation to our knowledge of

them those historical facts which are also themes of faith undergo a vigorous elaboration by which they take on appearances which they did not at first present. The Christ of faith, for example, is very different from the Christ of history. From the latter, faith has taken the nucleus and suggestion of a mystical and theological reconstruction ever higher and more comprehensive. But we must not suppose that from an ontological point of view the historical Christ did not include those ethical values and those religious meanings which Christian experience, by living the Gospel life, has slowly become aware of.

An example will clear our meaning. The mathematician, as such, may fail to perceive a harmony which is evident to the musician, but this does not mean that the harmony is not real or that the musician has created it. The musician finds it where the other fails to find it. So in our case. Religious facts include mysterious meanings which pure science misses. Faith, with its peculiar power, penetrates to these meanings and feeds on them. It does not create them; it finds them. But to find them we just need this faculty of faith which, working upon the facts, does undoubtedly transfigure and disfigure them, but only from the knowledge point of view and not ontologically. With this explanation of our position, the reproach of the Encyclical falls flat. For Modernism admits—what all must admit—the progress of our reflex knowledge of the supernatural; and it does not deny that dogma requires the rich fecundity of the initial fact upon which faith exercises its marvellous and inexplicable labour of vital assimilation.

An eloquent confirmation of this is supplied by what we have said above on the results of historical criticism as applied to Christianity.

Dogmatic thought has never gone beyond its assigned task of furnishing merely the formulas suitable to shape the moral attitude of the faithful according to the Gospel type of religious experience. The faithful Christian owed to Christ an attitude of obedience and affection due to one in whom dwelt the fulness of the divinity, and he owed to the Holy Spirit, by whom his soul was flooded with graces, an attitude of devotion as to one through whom, by an ineffable mystery, the divine life was transmitted to his soul. But how many vain essays before arriving at a less inexact representation of these mysteries—before establishing the definitions of Nicea! Alexandrine subordinationism, Sabellian modalism, which sacrificed the distinction of persons; Tertullian's Trinitarianism, which imperilled monotheism; Hippolytus' theory of two persons and a non-personal gift, the conflict between Denys of Rome and Denys of Alexandria—all these represent so many attempts made to arrive at a Trinitarian formula that should succeed in so affecting the moral life of the Christian as to determine its true religious attitute towards God the Father and Christ whom He has sent, and the Spirit who is the source of our supernatural life. *

* From the fact that Modernists deny that even our highest theological conceptions of Christ can be adequate or exhaustive, the Encyclical concludes that, "with sacrilegious audacity they degrade the Person of the Divine Redeemer to the condition of a simple and ordinary man."

This reckless and utterly false assertion has been taken up and reiterated by Mgr. Moyes in the *Nineteenth Century* for December, 1907, in an article designed to enlist Protestant sympathy by minimising and cloaking the anti-Protestant implications of the Encyclical, and by maximising the critical conclusions of the most extreme Modernists and ascribing them to the whole class. His methods, no less than his style, are those of his controversial school. He takes a premiss from some Modernist; combines it with one of his own, which the said Modernist denies, and then draws a conclusion which he accuses all Modernists of holding. This is not merely accusation on inference, but on false inference. Thus he does not attempt to adduce any passage from the more notorious Modernists such as Abbé Loisy, or M. Le Roy, or Father Tyrrell or Père Laberthonnière, denying the divinity of Christ. He knows very well that all these writers profess, whether logically or not, their belief in the Catholic faith, though they cannot possibly hold those conclusions of scholastic Christology, which are wrecked for ever by the established results of New Testament criticism. Of these results Mgr. Moyes professes to know nothing. Like the Encyclical he would have his simple-minded readers believe that Modernism is a wanton freak of *a priori* theologising, and not an honest attempt to reconcile Catholicism with whole masses of hard indigestible facts for which his own scholastic synthesis finds no room and no explanation. The truth is that for those who believe that certain purely historical facts and scientific truths are miraculously revealed, historical and scientific evidence can never yield more than provisional opinions, mutable at the command of

But all these doctrinal essays imply a transfiguration of the simple elements of the Gospel which is merely in the order of knowledge; for the underlying and unalterable dogmatic realities already included from the first all those religious values which little by little have become apparent through the reflection of faith.

---

authority. They do not see that such scepticism destroys the certitude of the fact of revelation and ends in blind fideism. Thus though the historical demonstrations of the limitations of Christ's human knowledge are stronger than those by which Mgr. Moyes would prove the fact of a revelation to the contrary, the former leave him unaffected. In the present instance his argument seems to be that many Modernists contend that Christ's human mind was incapable in the first moment of His conception of a clear consciousness of His hypostatic union, and that His Messianic self-consciousness grew with His growth in wisdom and stature. He then assumes, what no Modernist will admit, that to deny such consciousness is to deny the divinity of Christ; and at once asserts that all Modernists are guilty of this denial. Apparently he thinks that to be the Christ or to be the Son of God it is necessary to be aware of the fact. One might ask him: is the newly-baptised infant conscious of the grace of sonship; or even, is any man conscious of his full relationship to God in the natural or supernatural order? The excuse for these inferential accusations is that the whole syllogistic rigmarole of scholastic Christology perishes if one link in the chain be broken. Mgr. Moyes can of course afford to be reckless, knowing well that no Modernist can now reply to his travesties without incurring excommunication, and that he strikes an adversary who is bound hand and foot.—[Translator's Note.]

## PARTICULAR QUESTIONS

SO far we have only been explaining and defending our real positions against the false and biassed accusations of the Encyclical. But we are also there reproached with certain assertions, stigmatised as erroneous, which in reality are the authentic teachings of Catholic tradition, and in whose cause we must take the offensive against the papal document.

### SEC. I.—THE RELATIVE VALUE OF RELIGIONS

The Encyclical says: "Modernists do not deny, they even admit, some openly, others covertly, that all religions are true." Put thus absolutely the phrase may sound startling. But it does not represent our view. All we say is that every religion, if we consider the grade of culture and social development reached by its votaries, evokes a beneficial and salutary experience. Further we say that the relation between other religions, past and present, and Christianity is not one of equality, but one of the less perfect towards the more perfect. And in so saying we defy the compilers of the Encyclical to prove us at variance with the best testimony of the

Fathers and doctors of the Church. For all these agree in holding that the lower religions retain certain elements of goodness, inasmuch as each of them has assimilated some fragment of the primitive revelation.

Amongst the earliest Christian apologists S. Justin agreed with us when, appropriating the stoic notion of the λόγος σπερματικὸς, he explained it as a reason or knowledge whose germ was implanted by God in *every* soul; or when, turning to the pagans, he said: "We declare that Jesus Christ is the Logos, *the Logos whereof the whole human race is partaker;* and that those men who have lived according to the Logos (Reason) are Christians, even though they be reckoned among atheists. Such among the Greeks were Socrates, Heraclitus and their like; and among the barbarians, Abraham, Ananiah, Azariah, Misael, and Elijah. All those who now live according to the Logos are Christians. . . . The teachings of Plato do not contradict those of Christ, and the same is to be said of the stoics and the poets. Each has had a partial vision of the divine all-pervading reason. All the truths they have proclaimed belong to us Christians."* Athenagoras affirmed that all men "by obeying an inspiration that comes from God" agree as to certain fundamental religious beliefs.† Clement of Alexandria gives us some won-

* *Apol.* I° and II°. † *Ap.* 7.

derful reflections to the point: "Let us apply the parable of the sower as interpreted for us by the Saviour Himself (Matt. xiii). For this field, which is mankind, there is but one Husbandman. From the beginning of the world this Husbandman sows the life-giving seed and waters it at all times with the rain of His Word. But the diverse times and places in which the Word is received cause a diversity of results. . . . There was an ancient and natural converse between man and heaven. The Word has never been hidden from anyone. He is the universal light shining upon all men. The manifestation of the divine unity and the divine omnipotence is in all upright men a natural thing.* S. Augustine too affirms the spontaneity or naturalness of the religious sentiment in all positive forms, and goes so far as to say, with the platonists, that our knowledge of God is simply a remembering. And in this he is followed by S. Anselm, who teaches that our spiritual labour of reflection and thought aims at bringing out into distinctive relief the divine image naturally stamped on the soul.

But we forbear to multiply testimonies which for the most part would coincide with those which we have adduced already, and might still adduce, in favour of the immanence of religion.

---

* *Strom.* i. 5, 17; vi. 8, 9: v. 13.

## SEC. 2.—SCIENCE AND FAITH

With a decidedly halting logic the Encyclical accuses Modernism at once of separating science from faith and of subjecting faith to science "in three ways: because every religious fact falls under the jurisdiction of science; because the very idea of God is subject to science; and because the believer feels inwardly constrained to bring Faith and Science into accord." And so the papal document applies to Modernists the words with which Gregory IX. rebuked certain doctors of theology for twisting "the heavenly pages of the Bible into agreement with philosophical theories."* The very contradictoriness of the rebuke is enough to show its futility. As we have already said, Modernists, in full agreement with contemporary psychology, dis-

* This letter of Gregory IX. is of 1228, and not of 1223, as the Encyclical supposes, misled by Denziger's *Enchiridion*, from which, and not from its original source and context, it quotes the passage. But this matters little, Had the compiler of the Encyclical gone to the source and context he would have seen that the violent words of Gregory were directed against the scholastics of the university of Paris, who, like their descendants, were wont to use Scripture texts uncritically in support of their metaphysical placets. Yet it is these scholastics and their uncritical apriorist method whom the Encyclical *Pascendi* extols at the expense of those who would now deliver the Scriptures from such perverse handling. As an attempt to express Christian experience in the philosophical language of that day, scholasticism, with all its limitations, was the mediæval Modernism, and as such could not be suppressed, as we see, not only from subsequent history, but also from another letter of Gregory IX. in 1231, which practically unsays what he had said in 1228.

tinguish sharply between science and faith. The spiritual sources from which they proceed seem to us quite distinct and independent. This, for us, is a fundamental acquisition. The pretence that we subjugate faith to science is simply senseless. If the outward expressions of individual and collective faith, if theological systems are facts which as such come under the domain of science, this does not in any way mean that the underlying psychological movement, called faith, is tied to or dependent on scientific theories. Criticism analyses the outward forms and the public affirmations of faith. But religious faith itself, that instinctive need of every healthy mind, although in its reflex self-consciousness and self-expression it may be affected by general culture, springs up spontaneously in the soul and expands itself independently of all scientific training. And so, instead of taking the words of Gregory IX. as applicable to ourselves, we can turn them against the theologians who have always misused Scripture and travestied its genuine sense in support of their foregone conclusions. Modernists, on the contrary, instead of twisting the Bible in the interests of a somewhat disingenuous apologetic, make a sharp distinction in the sacred documents between the historical foundation and the expression of religious faith. And hence they examine them with two faculties: the scientific faculty, which, by use of proper historical methods, estimates the value of the scriptural sources as those of any other historical documents; and the faculty of faith, or religious intuition, which strives, by assimilation and sympathetic self-adaptation, to re-experience in itself that religious experience of which the Bible is the written record.

### SEC. 3.—CHURCH AND STATE

Finally, the Encyclical reprehends our desire to separate Church and State. Here, again, the official Church counts as a fault what is one of our best aspirations—one which she herself would welcome, were it not that her vision of facts is clouded by her ties and attachments to the worldly splendour which she enjoyed in a past age that can never come back again.

We quite understand those decisive practical reasons that moved the Church in the Middle Ages to take to herself a political power which, however it may at times have hampered her spiritual influence, did, nevertheless, further the development of mediæval Europe in some ways. But the historical conditions which induced the Church to assume a political responsibility separable from, if not quite incompatible with, her spiritual power, have long ceased to exist. The modern State is accepted as the instrument destined to regulate the development of the community in material and moral interests, so far as these affect the public life. It has a well-defined programme and ample means of government. Things being so the Church should be only too glad to be able to lay down every sort of political preoccupation, and to retire back into the sphere of her spiritual dominion, confining herself to the religious guidance of souls. For her specific aims she has everything to gain from this separation of powers. What sort of sympathy is she likely to win from the best spirits of the age by these wretched remnants of a power that she has lost, or by her vain efforts to re-acquire it? What sort of popularity can these dwindling and decrepit aristocratic oligarchies confer upon her which, in exchange for a little paltry grandeur, would tie her to customs in open discord with modern tendencies? One thing we know, and we say it openly: we know that we are weary of seeing the Church reduced, for all practical purposes, to a bureaucracy jealous of its surviving scraps of political power and hungering to get back all it once had—to a group of idle men who, having dedicated themselves to a priestly and apostolic calling, and having afterwards attained the highest ecclesiastical grade, enjoy the most fabulously wealthy benefices as absentee incumbents. We are weary of seeing her reduced to a sterilised force, which, notwithstanding an apparent grandeur that wins the facile and unintelligent adulation of the multitude, acts as a brake on social progress; to an institution which squanders its vital energy in idly dreaming of what it used to be in ages gone by. We see no other effectual way of ending this miserable state of things than the entire separation of the Church from political functions; the return to the simpler religion that will throw open the doors of the Church to the excluded democracy and enable her to pour out upon it those treasured riches of spirituality which the Christian tradition has stored in her bosom. Away, then, with all these empty political ambitions; away with all this plotting to reconstitute, on different but equivalent lines, that civil power which the Church exercised in the Middle Ages. Let the Church learn to be once more that great moral force which she was in her less imposing but more fruitful periods, and especially in her primitive days, and her history, which to-day traces the course of a parabolic descent, will receive a new and vigorous upward impulse. The Church should feel a sort of nostalgia, a yearning towards her own past, in regard to those, as yet unconsciously religious, currents of thought and sentiment which are the life-blood of the rising democracy. She should find some way of mingling with this world-movement in order to ensure its true success by means of the strength of her restraints and the stimulus of her moral authority, which alone can bring home the lessons of self-denial and altruism to the multitudes. She should frankly recognise that democracy paves the way to what is precisely the highest expression of her Catholicism. When she does so, then democracy will begin to yearn after the Church which continues that Gospel-message wherein democracy finds its own remote but authentic origin.

## SEC. 4.—RESUMÉ.

"If we take in the whole system [of Modernism] at one glance no one will be surprised when we define it as the synthesis of all heresies." So the Encyclical gathers up its charges against Modernism and were its premises only true its conclusion would be fully justified. If Modernism were, as it says, saturated with agnosticism it would tear away the basis of Catholic faith and open the road to atheism. In the foregoing pages we have tried to show that it is far otherwise. Undoubtedly a crisis has arisen in the very centre of Catholic thought—a crisis that affects no one particular dogma, but extends to the whole general attitude to be taken as to the traditional idea of revelation and of the supernatural, and as to the whole complexus of data presented to us by Catholicism. One who sets out with the idea that Christianity and its scholastic interpretation are one and the same thing may well see in Modernism, which is essentially critical and anti-scholastic, a very grave danger to the integrity of the Christian tradition. But such childish fears are far from those who see that, besides scholasticism, there are other systems of thought into which the Gospel experiences can be translated. History shows us many a great crisis like the present which has arisen in the Church from the need of adapting faith to the current forms of philosophy and social organisation, and which has issued to the Church's advantage, enabling her to come out of the conflict with a higher consciousness and expression of her own nature.

Heresy and schism have always been the results of some partial dispute about a particular dogma or placet of authority, In the history of the Church we can always verify the strange paradox that doctrinal crises have ever been settled more peaceably in the measure that larger and more universal principles were affected by them, and that, contrariwise, they have given birth to more lamentable divisions in the measure that the point at issue was of narrower interest.

Hence we may rightly augur that our own movement, being so wide-reaching and complex in its consequences, will triumph without any violent cataclysm, that it will quietly absorb and be absorbed by the Church.

## THE CAMPAIGN AGAINST MODERNISM

THE part which concerns the measures to be taken against Modernism is the most serious, and, in the judgment of all, the least commendable part of the whole Encyclical. Pius X. ordains that all the young professors suspected of Modernism (and they are not a few) are to be driven from their chairs in the seminaries; that infected books are to be condemned indiscriminately, even though they may have received an *imprimatur;* that a committee of safe censors for the revision of books is to be established in every diocese; that meetings of modernising priests or laymen are to be forbidden; that young ecclesiastics who seem anxious to follow and study the general movement of contemporary thought are to be prevented from so doing; that every diocese is to have a vigilance committee to discover and delate Modernists; and that finally bishops are to inform the Holy See periodically on the condition of their respective dioceses in regard to the spread of Modernist ideas.

However inclined we may be to receive the word of the Pope respectfully, we cannot bring ourselves to see in these disciplinary measures that calm and gentle spirit which should reign in the heart of one who speaks in the name of Christ. Such measures represent the extremest length to which rigour and severity dare go in this twentieth century, no longer tolerant of more barbarous customs. They even revive in some particulars the excesses of the mediæval Inquisition—nay more, they equal the extravagances for which Julian the apostate has been so often condemned who excluded Christian teachers from the schools. What else can it be called but an outburst of anger which orders the young clerical Modernists, that is to say, the most capable and industrious, to be repulsed, to be put in the lowest places, to have their faculties sterilised, to be held up to the contempt of their less capable but more servile and obsequious comrades?

Some of the above measures not only display an unseasonable and excessive rigour, but also defy fundamental principles of canon law. The committees of vigilance, for instance, tend to circumscribe episcopal authority and to breed resentment and divisions in the ranks of the clergy by making every cleric suspicious of his fellow, who may be, for aught he knows, a spy, and by opening the road to all sorts of mischief and unworthy reprisals. Further, to allow works to be condemned in one diocese which are authorised in another, besides favouring the monstrous and grotesque idea that truth differs for different dioceses, discredits the authority of the revisers and brings it into public contempt. The secrecy to be observed as to the censor's name is not only impracticable, but has the grave inconvenience of accentuating one of the most intolerable abuses which the Church has inherited from the Middle Ages—that of passing sentence in intellectual matters without assigning any reasons. Finally, the gagging of the Catholic press can only result in limiting its public influence.

Taken all together, these measures not only bear scant witness to the magnanimity of whoever has devised them, but also show what a vain terror Modernism has aroused in the upper ranks of the hierarchy. Instead of letting the conflict work itself out quietly, and the solution appear in due course, the movement is to be violently arrested and draconian laws are to be enacted against us. For our part, we have no desire that our opponents should be forbidden to express their ideas, since we have too much confidence in the soundness of our cause to stand in fear of discussion. We cannot but remind the Vatican of the words of Gamaliel to the Pharisees who were for imprisoning Peter and his companions: "Let these men go free. For if their work be of men it will come to naught, but if it be of God, ye cannot overthrow it, lest haply ye be found to fight against God" (Acts v. 38).

We ask Pius X. to repeat this experiment and to let us go free and continue our work, even as the Pharisees allowed the Apostles to do. If our work has life in it, it will triumph in spite of persecutions, though not to the credit of the persecutors; if it is artificial and sterilising it will inevitably come to naught.

## CONCLUSION

AND now let us conclude, speaking, as all along we have spoken, calmly and without anger, mindful of the words "non in commotione Dominus"—God is a God of peace.

A great spiritual crisis, which did not begin to-day, but has to-day reached its culminating intensity, troubles all the religious bodies of Europe—Catholicism, Lutheranism, Anglicanism. For the most part it is due to the new orientation of the public mind, which is adverse to the traditional formulation of the religious spirit; it is due to the easily-popularised results of science, which diffuse an instinctive distrust of those metaphysical and historical titles on which the dogmatic teaching of the Churches rests its claims. Catholicism, by reason of its greater antiquity and of the more tenaciously guarded elements of mediævalism within its system, and, at the same time, by reason of its more direct opposition to the affirmations of science and to the will of the democracy, feels the pain and distress of the profound crisis more acutely. But manifestly it will not be able to eliminate science or to stifle democracy with the barren words of its condemnations or with the noisy terrors of its anathemas. The movements of thought in an age like ours, where culture is so deep-rooted and widespread, is no slender rill to be easily dammed and arrested in its course. It is an irresistible tide whose advance authority should wisely direct and not foolishly try to obstruct. If the successor of Peter condemns, with such unwonted asperity, the science and the apologetic of our times, we ask ourselves whether this may not be due to some understandable ignorance of the tendencies that characterise the moral evolution of to-day, as well as to a radical inability to foresee the success which inevitably must crown the progressive efforts of the modern world. By our familiarity with such numbers and numbers of the ecclesiastical hierarchy we know very well how the clerical generation of the immediate past was perversely educated in the most cordial contempt of modern culture, and also, it must be confessed, in a most monstrous esteem of its own mediæval theological education. We have often reflected on the strange spectacle offered by these out-of-date individuals who live in contact with the modern world without any understanding of its aspirations, its ideals, its language. But this section of the clergy which at present occupies nearly all the leading positions of the hierarchy should not be a hindrance to us who, after having received our scholastic education, have set to work to master that language, to grasp those ideals, to complete the reconciliation of the old Catholic tradition with the new thought and the new social aspirations. Through living, and not merely local, contact with the world in which we dwell we have come to dream of a great unification; we have grown to a conviction that even the most revolutionary pronouncements of science can in no wise upset the affirmation of religious faith, since the spiritual processes from which faith and science result are independent of one another and the laws of their development wholly different. We are convinced that the fundamental aspirations of democracy—of this collective and altruistic movement towards a fuller realisation of justice among men—contain a religious element closely and strangely akin to the Messianic hope by which Christ bound His followers in the bonds of fraternity. Strong in this conviction we had girt ourselves for the task of bringing the religious experience of Christianity into line with the data of contemporary science and philosophy and of emphasising the religious and Christian elements that go to the constitution of the democratic movement. But now ecclesiastical authority brusquely arrests our progress and condemns our labours. Well, we feel that it is our duty to offer a loyal resistance, and at any cost to defend that Catholic tradition, whereof the

Church is guardian, in a way which for the moment may merit the condemnation of authority, but which, we are sure, will in the end prevail to the Church's advantage.

It is said, or course, that our opinions are incompatible with Catholic teaching, and that if accepted they would ruin the Church. In the foregoing pages we sought to show the idleness of such fears; we have even proved that the substance of our thought (stripped of those exaggerations and inaccuracies which only a controversialist's desire to discredit our movement could ascribe to us) is simply a return to certain half-forgotten principles of which Christian apologetic, in its golden age and prior to scholasticism, had always made use. But besides this demonstration of the legitimacy of our religious and intellectual positions we can also adduce an indirect argument which we develop here because it is the most triumphant answer to those who say that our movement is hurtful to Catholicism from the doctrinal and hierarchical point of view. It is this: In every crisis which Christianity has passed through in the course of its development, and whenever the opposition between past and unyielding forms of religious expression and a new culture to which they are unsuited has become acute, there has arisen in the Church a handful of men animated with the design of reconciling the old piety, unchangeable in its simplicity as a spiritual fact, with the new modes of thought. And at the same time the voice of the timorous and faithless has ever been raised with pitiable cowardice to denounce their courageous enterprise as heralding disruption and calamity. The effects of this conflict have been always advantageous in the same way. The timorous have exercised a providential restraint on the hardihood of the courageous, apt to run to excess in one direction or another. But after this period of wavering and hesitation, and as soon as the advantages of the new method over the old became evident, the bulk of the faithful have sided gladly and fearlessly with those who had formerly been denounced as revolutionaries. Examples abound in Church history. We may cite one or two of the more remarkable.

When at the close of the second century Gnosticism, with the refinements of its theosophic speculation, robbed the Church of some of her best and most cultured proselytes, whose minds could not easily rest in the rude and simple piety of the faithful, it became for some Christian thinkers a problem of life and death whether Christianity ought absolutely to refuse the aid of the classical philosophy, and so lose its strongest hold on the educated classes, or ought rather studiously to seek some way of reconciling the splendid tradition of classical philosophy with the new spirit of the Gospel. Up to that time, those who had sought such a reconciliation had ended by sacrificing the Gospel to philosophy and so spoiling it of all its originality; and this fact had given the mass of the faithful a profound distrust of philosophy; while the Gnostics, who were responsible for this hasty and violent synthesis, withdrew altogether from the official Church.

But this passive distrust was no solution of the problem which thrust itself irrepressibly on the attention of those who regarded the Church as a force capable of development and diffusion, and who felt grieved at the scanty success of her propaganda in the centres of culture. Amongst these men, Clement, who presided over the catechetical school of Alexandria, boldly undertook to demonstrate not only the compatibility but the intimate correlation and affinity between pagan philosophy and Christianity. What happened? His project was so opposed by his fellow-believers that his great trilogy which passed step by step from the ethical preparation for religion to a rational demonstration of the faith, remained unfinished, and the third and most important part was replaced by that somewhat fantastic composition, allegorically called *Stromateis*, in which the illustrious Alexandrian tried to show the rectitude of his intention and the orthodoxy of his views. This work is accompanied with certain vague remonstrances addressed to his "simple" co-religionists, who would discredit his enterprise, and who go about belittling the value of philosophical apologetic. "According to these men," he says, "it is useless to write books. But if bad men, whose writings destroy the souls of their readers, write books, shall he who makes known the truth be forbidden to do so? It is a useful thing to beget good children. But a man's writings are the children begotten by his spirit."* And elsewhere: "There are some of us who reject philosophy, and would have us contend with pure and simple faith. But that were to look for grapes at once before training the vine."† Might not such words be applied to those who denounce Modernism, whose only crime is that of trying to find a path for faith through the critical and philosophical embarrassments created for it by contemporary thought? But in spite of momentary opposition Clement's programme of a fusion of classical philosophy and Christian beliefs triumphed in the end and became the official apologetic of Catholicism. The Church showed herself to be a social organism, gifted with the infallible instinct of every living thing, by which, after a period of hesitation and experiment, she discovers those solutions which are essential for her existence.

Another most significant example of the struggles

* *Strom.* i. 1. † *Strom.* i. 4.

to be faced by all those who, having studied the requirements of the time, strive to adapt the Church accordingly, is afforded by that very scholasticism which to-day is such an undeniable encumbrance to the progress of Catholicism, but which in its own day represented a vigorous revolutionary movement against the philosophical tradition of the Fathers, and was held for such by the Roman Pontiffs. Aristotle, of whose riches S. Thomas has made such spoil, was little known in the later Middle Ages. It was only the Arabian philosophers who brought his more important works to the knowledge of the West. The first mention of them occurs in 1210, and that in a provincial synod held at Paris, when it was decreed that "neither the works of Aristotle concerning natural philosophy, nor any commentary thereon, is to be read at Paris, whether privately or publicly." In 1228 Gregory IX. approved and appropriated this condemnation, and again, though with considerable mitigations, in 1231. Once more, in 1263, Urban IV. renewed the prohibition, doomed, however, to failure in face of the irresistible tendency of the time, which found in the Aristotelian metaphysics the most satisfactory formulation of its own views of reality, and which therefore tried to adopt it, and to attune it to that Catholic dogma which, in its turn, had been the expression of Christian piety arrived at full self-consciousness. The great artificer of this labour of harmonisation was S. Thomas Aquinas, distrusted at first by his colleagues and superiors on account of his Aristotelian sympathies; authorised later, only by special papal permission, to study that philosophy; ultimately triumphant in his *Summa Theologica*—that perfect synthesis of dogma with Aristotelian method and metaphysic. S. Thomas was thus the true Modernist of his time, the man who strove with marvellous perseverance and genius to harmonise his faith with the thought of that day. And we are the true successors of the scholastics in all that was valuable in their work—in their keen sense of the adaptability of the Christian religion to the ever-changing forms of philosophy and general culture.

These and like examples are full of auguries for our future. They bid us hope that our work, too, though at present abused and condemned, may one day be justly appreciated, and that the Church may draw from it those advantages which we, her loyal and disinterested servants, have had in view. Ideas move slowly, and if we should never live to enjoy the crowning of our labours, if the slow process of religious revival should be too gradual for us to be able to see the issue, we shall not grieve on that account, accustomed as we are to hide our personality behind that idea of which we are the unworthy champions; nor shall we ever lose confidence. We have cast the seed in the furrow; Time will do the rest.

Very likely this unconquerable confidence in the success of our work will be taken as a new proof of our pride and obstinacy. Indeed, we have had heavier reproaches heaped on us. The Encyclical goes so far as to call us "enemies of the Cross of Christ, who labour for the downfall of the kingdom of Jesus Christ." Of all the phrases of the papal document this is the one which, falling from the lips of our father, has caused us the most poignant grief. We do not want to make declarations that would redound ever so remotely to our own praise. But since we ourselves are not in cause, nor are we seeking our own honour, but that of the truths which these pages present to the world, and since the Gospel has said, "By their fruits ye shall know them," we may not shrink from the duty of protesting against the bitter reproof. If there is anything that fires our life with an enthusiasm, for which the Encyclical might at least have shown some respect, it is the desire to spread the kingdom of Christ, to secure for it an ampler, more living, more conspicuous triumph upon earth. And yet the Encyclical holds us up to the disdain of the faithful as blasphemers of the Cross! We, on the contrary, are conscious of being the most ardent champions of its universal honour.

Long and painful were those periods of perplexity through which we passed when honest scientific research first brought down about our ears the artificial structure of the scholastic interpretation of Catholicism. Our faith did not fail us in that hour, but trusting in the infallible harmony between the truth of faith and the truth of reason, and turning back to the pure sources of Christianity, we attempted to find a new synthesis. Once in view of it, we tried to formulate it and impart it to our brethren, to whom the language of scholasticism has become permanently and incurably incomprehensible.

We have gained no honour from our apostolate, but rather persecutions (moral and material), disillusions and bitter conflicts. But we have ever kept before us the evangelical precept which bids us instantly sacrifice our dearest private interests for the kingdom of God. Our life has been, and is still, spent in a weary effort to bring all the spiritual energies of men to co-operate with that divine will which realises itself progressively in the world. And therefore we believe we have full rights of citizenship in the Catholic Church; we believe that we are its most devoted and loving sons. Do we not hold ourselves, and seek to revive in others, the purest traditions of Christianity? Christianity has, in fact, been, in its origin and in its most flourishing period, a powerful stimulus and a profound hope, through which souls have been raised to a nobler conception of life, and to a more intense and disinterested activity for the common good. We would fain see it once more a force of progress in the world. And therefore we desire that, at a time when contemporary civilisation, saturated with the scientific spirit and eager with democratic aspirations, is groping after a higher experience of the Christian religion, the Cross of Christ should not be invoked against the spread of truth and light, and that it should not be dragged into bitter political strife against the inevitable ascendancy of the democracy—against the deposition of the mighty and the exaltation of the lowly.

What appeals to us and cheers us on is the ideal of a Church restored to her office as guide of souls in their weary pilgrimage to the distant goal towards which they are spurred by the Spirit of God—a spirit of brotherhood and of peace. All our efforts are directed to inspiring souls with this renewed sense of the imperishable destinies of Catholicism in the world. The momentary condemnation of these efforts does not discourage us. Even were the official Church, in its blindness to the righteousness of our aims, to repel us more roughly and violently than it has already done, we should abide untroubled in conscience, remembering those illuminating words of S. Augustine,* with which we conclude our defence:

"Divine Providence often allows even good men to be driven out of the Church by the turbulence and intrigues of the carnal-minded. And if they bear this insult and injury patiently for the peace of the Church, and do not start some new schism or heresy, they will teach men with what affection and sincerity of love God is to be served. The fixed purpose of such men is to return as soon as ever the storm is over; or, if that is not possible—either because the same tempest continues, or because their return would raise another as bad, or worse—they resolve to work for the good of those very men of whose turbulence they are the victims, never forming a separate congregation, defending unto death and aiding by their testimony that faith which they know to be preached in the Catholic Church. These the Father, who sees in secret, crowns in

* "Saepe etiam sinit divina providentia, per nonnullas nimium turbulentas carnalium hominum seditiones, expelli de congregatione Christiana, etiam bonos viros. Quam contumeliam vel injuriam suam cum patientissime pro ecclesiae pace tulerint, neque ullas novitates, vel schismatis vel haeresis, moliti fuerint, docebunt homines quam vero affectu, et quanta sinceritate charitatis Deo serviendum sit. Talium ergo virorum propositum est, aut sedatis remeare turbinibus; aut si id non sinantur (vel eadem tempestate perseverante, vel ne suo reditu talis aut saevior oriatur) tenent voluntatem consulendi etiam eis ipsis quorum motibus perturbationibusque cesserunt, sine ulla conventiculorum segregatione usque ad mortem defendentes et testimonio juvantes eam fidem quam in ecclesia

secret. It seems a rare case, but examples are not wanting—nay, they are more numerous than commonly supposed."

---

catholica praedicari sciunt. Hos coronat in occulto Pater, in occulto videns. Rarum hoc videtur genus ; sed tamen exempla non desunt ; imo plura sunt quam credi potest."

S. Augustine, *De Vera Religione*, c. vi. (Ed. Maur, vol. i. p. 751, col. 1 C. D. col. 2 A.)

# ENCYCLICAL LETTER

## ("*Pascendi Gregis*")

Of our most Holy Lord, PIUS X., by Divine Providence Pope, on the Doctrines of the Modernists

*To the Patriarchs, Primates, Archbishops, and other Local Ordinaries in Peace and Communion with the Apostolic See.*

### POPE PIUS X

VENERABLE BRETHREN, HEALTH AND THE APOSTOLIC BENEDICTION

ONE of the primary obligations assigned by Christ to the office divinely committed to Us of feeding the Lord's flock is that of guarding with the greatest vigilance the deposit of the faith delivered to the saints, rejecting the profane novelties of words and the gainsaying of knowledge falsely so called. There has never been a time when this watchfulness of the supreme pastor was not necessary to the Catholic body; for, owing to the efforts of the enemy of the human race, there have never been lacking "men speaking perverse things" (Acts xx. 30), "vain talkers and seducers" (Tit. i. 10), "erring and driving into error" (2 Tim. iii. 13). It must, however, be confessed that these latter days have witnessed a notable increase in the number of the enemies of the Cross of Christ, who, by arts entirely new and full of deceit, are striving to destroy the vital energy of the Church, and, as far as in them lies, utterly to subvert the very Kingdom of Christ. Wherefore We may no longer keep silence, lest We should seem to fail in Our most sacred duty, and lest the kindness that, in the hope of wiser counsels, We have hitherto shown them, should be set down to lack of diligence in the discharge of Our office.

### [GRAVITY OF THE SITUATION]*

That We should act without delay in this matter is made imperative especially by the fact that the partisans of error are to be sought not only among the Church's open enemies; but, what is to be most dreaded and deplored, in her very bosom, and are

---

* These headings in brackets are not in the original, and are inserted for the convenience of the reader.

the more mischievous the less they keep in the open. We allude, Venerable Brethren, to many who belong to the Catholic laity, and, what is much more sad, to the ranks of the priesthood itself, who, animated by a false zeal for the Church, lacking the solid safeguards of philosophy and theology, nay more, thoroughly imbued with the poisonous doctrines taught by the enemies of the Church, and lost to all sense of modesty, put themselves forward as reformers of the Church; and, forming more boldly into line of attack, assail all that is most sacred in the work of Christ, not sparing even the Person of the Divine Redeemer, Whom, with sacrilegious audacity, they degrade to the condition of a simple and ordinary man.

Although they express their astonishment that We should number them amongst the enemies of the Church, no one will be reasonably surprised that We should do so, if, leaving out of account the internal disposition of the soul, of which God alone is the Judge, he considers their tenets, their manner of speech, and their action. Nor indeed would he be wrong in regarding them as the most pernicious of all the adversaries of the Church. For, as We have said, they put into operation their designs for her undoing, not from without but from within. Hence, the danger is present almost in the very veins and heart of the Church, whose injury is the more certain from the very fact that their knowledge of her is more intimate. Moreover, they lay the axe not to the branches and shoots, but to the very root, that is, to the faith and its deepest fibres. And once having struck at this root of immortality, they proceed to diffuse poison through the whole tree, so that there is no part of Catholic truth which they leave untouched, none that they do not strive to corrupt. Further, none is more skilful, none more astute than they, in the employment of a thousand noxious devices; for they play the double part of rationalist and Catholic, and this so craftily that they easily lead the unwary into error; and as audacity is their chief characteristic, there is no conclusion of any kind from which they shrink or which they do not thrust forward with pertinacity and assurance. To this must be added the fact, which indeed is well calculated to deceive souls, that they lead a life of the greatest activity, of assiduous and ardent application to every branch of learning, and that they possess, as a rule, a reputation for irreproachable morality. Finally, there is the fact which is all but fatal to the hope of cure that their very doctrines have given such a bent to their minds, that they disdain all authority and brook no restraint; and relying upon a false conscience, they attempt to ascribe to a love of truth that which is in reality the result of pride and obstinacy.

Once indeed We had hopes of recalling them to a better mind, and to this end We first of all treated them with kindness as Our children, then with severity; and at last We have had recourse, though with great reluctance, to public reproof. It is known to you, Venerable Brethren, how unavailing have been our efforts. For a moment they have bowed their head, only to lift it more arrogantly than before. If it were a matter which concerned them alone, We might perhaps have overlooked it; but the security of the Catholic name is at stake. Wherefore We must interrupt a silence which it would be criminal to prolong, that We may point out to the whole Church, as they really are, men who are badly disguised.

### [DIVISION OF THE ENCYCLICAL]

It is one of the cleverest devices of the Modernists (as they are commonly and rightly called) to present their doctrines without order and systematic arrangement, in a scattered and disjointed manner, so as to make it appear as if their minds were in doubt or hesitation, whereas in reality they are quite fixed and steadfast. For this reason it will be of advantage, Venerable Brethren, to bring their teachings together here into one group, and to point out their interconnection, and thus to pass to an examination of the sources of the errors, and to prescribe remedies for averting the evil results.

## [PART I.: ANALYSIS OF MODERNIST TEACHING]

To proceed in an orderly manner in this somewhat abstruse subject, it must first of all be noted that the Modernist sustains and includes within himself a manifold personality; he is a philosopher, a believer, a theologian, an historian, a critic, an apologist, a reformer. These rôles must be clearly distinguished one from another by all who would accurately understand their system and thoroughly grasp the principles and the outcome of their doctrines.

### [AGNOSTICISM ITS PHILOSOPHICAL FOUNDATION]

We begin, then, with the philosopher. Modernists place the foundation of religious philosophy in that doctrine which is commonly called *Agnosticism*. According to this teaching human reason is confined entirely within the field of *phenomena*, that is to say, to things that appear, and in the manner in which they appear: it has neither the right nor the power to overstep these limits. Hence it is incapable of lifting itself up to God, and of recognising His existence, even by means of visible things. From this it is inferred that God can never be the direct object of science, and that, as regards history, He must not be considered as an historical subject. Given these premises, every one will at once perceive what becomes of *Natural Theology*, of the *motives of credibility*, of *external revelation.* The Modernists simply sweep them entirely aside; they include them in *Intellectualism* which they denounce as a system which is ridiculous and long since defunct. Nor does the fact that the Church has formally condemned these portentous errors exercise the slightest restraint upon them. Yet the Vatican Council has defined, "If anyone says that the one true God, our Creator and Lord, cannot be known with certainty by the natural light of human reason by means of the things that are made, let him be anathema;" * and also: "If anyone says that it is not possible or not expedient that man be taught, through the medium of divine revelation, about God and the worship to be paid Him, let him be anathema;" † and finally, "If anyone says that divine revelation cannot be made credible by external signs, and that therefore men should be drawn to the faith only by their personal internal experience or by private inspiration, let him be anathema." ‡ It may be asked, in what way do the Modernists contrive to make the transition from *Agnosticism*, which is a state of pure nescience, to scientific and historic *Atheism*, which is a doctrine of positive denial;

* *De Revel.*, can. 1. † *Ibid.*, can. 2. ‡ *De Fide.*, can. 3.

and consequently, by what legitimate process of reasoning, they proceed from the fact of ignorance as to whether God has in fact intervened in the history of the human race or not, to explain this history, leaving God out altogether, as if He really had not intervened. Let him answer who can. Yet it is a fixed and established principle among them that both science and history must be atheistic; and within their boundaries there is room for nothing but *phenomena;* God and all that is divine are utterly excluded. We shall soon see clearly what, as a consequence of this most absurd teaching, must be held touching the most sacred Person of Christ, and the mysteries of His life and death, and of His Resurrection and Ascension into Heaven.

### [VITAL IMMANENCE]

However, this *Agnosticism* is only the negative part of the system of the Modernists: the positive part consists in what they call *vital immanence.* Thus they advance from one to the other. Religion, whether natural or supernatural, must, like every other fact, admit of some explanation. But when natural theology has been destroyed, and the road to revelation closed by the rejection of the arguments of credibility, and all external revelation absolutely denied, it is clear that this explanation will be sought in vain outside of man himself. It must, therefore, be looked for *in* man; and since religion is a form of life, the explanation must certainly be found in the life of man. In this way is formulated the principle of *religious immanence*. Moreover, the first actuation, so to speak, of every vital phenomenon—and religion, as noted above, belongs to this category— is due to a certain need or impulsion; but speaking more particularly of life, it has its origin in a movement of the heart, which movement is called a *sense*. Therefore, as God is the object of religion, we must conclude that faith, which is the basis and foundation of all religion, must consist in a certain interior sense, originating in a need of the divine. This need of the divine, which is experienced only in special and favourable circumstances, cannot, of itself, appertain to the domain of consciousness,* but is first latent beneath consciousness, or, to borrow a term from modern philosophy, in the *subconsciousness*, where also its root lies hidden and undetected.

It may perhaps be asked how it is that this need of the divine which man experiences within himself resolves itself into religion? To this question the Modernist reply would be as follows: Science and

* [In the Latin text the word is *conscientia*, which may be rendered in English as "conscience" or "consciousness," and in the present translation it is so used as the context seems to require.—*Translator's note.*]

history are confined within two boundaries, the one external, namely, the visible world, the other internal, which is consciousness. When one or other of these limits has been reached, there can be no further progress, for beyond is the *unknowable*. In presence of this *unknowable*, whether it is outside man and beyond the visible world of nature, or lies hidden within the *subconsciousness*, the need of the divine in a soul which is prone to religion, excites—according to the principles of *Fideism*, without any previous advertence of the mind—a certain special *sense*, and this sense possesses, implied within itself both as its own object and as its intrinsic cause, the divine *reality* itself, and in a way unites man with God. It is this *sense* to which Modernists give the name of faith, and this is what they hold to be the beginning of religion.

But we have not yet reached the end of their philosophising, or, to speak more accurately, of their folly. Modernists find in this *sense*, not only faith, but in and with faith, as they understand it, they affirm that there is also to be found *revelation*. For, indeed, what more is needed to constitute a revelation? Is not that religious *sense* which is perceptible in the conscience, revelation, or at least the beginning of revelation? Nay, is it not God Himself manifesting Himself, indistinctly, it is true, in this same religious *sense*, to the soul? And they add:

Since God is both the object and the cause of faith, this revelation is at the same time *of* God and *from* God, that is to say, God is both the Revealer and the Revealed.

From this, Venerable Brethren, springs that most absurd tenet of the Modernists, that every religion, according to the different aspect under which it is viewed, must be considered as both natural and supernatural. It is thus that they make consciousness and revelation synonymous. From this they derive the law laid down as the universal standard, according to which *religious consciousness* is to be put on an equal footing with revelation, and that to it all must submit, even the supreme authority of the Church, whether in the capacity of teacher, or in that of legislator in the province of sacred liturgy or discipline.

### [DEFORMATION OF RELIGIOUS HISTORY THE CONSEQUENCE ]

In all this process, from which, according to the Modernists, faith and revelation spring, one point is to be particularly noted, for it is of capital importance on account of the historico-critical corollaries which they deduce from it. The *Unknowable* they speak of does not present itself to faith as something solitary and isolated; but on the contrary in close conjunction with some phenomenon, which, though it belongs to the realms of science or history, yet to some extent exceeds their limits. Such a phenomenon may be a fact of nature containing within itself something mysterious; or it may be a man, whose character, actions, and words cannot, apparently, be reconciled with the ordinary laws of history. Then faith, attracted by the *Unknowable* which is united with the phenomenon, seizes upon the whole phenomenon, and, as it were, permeates it with its own life. From this two things follow. The first is a sort of *transfiguration* of the phenomenon by its elevation above its own true conditions, an elevation by which it becomes more adapted to clothe itself with the form of the divine character which faith will bestow upon it. The second consequence is a certain *disfiguration*—so it may be called—of the same phenomenon, arising from the fact that faith attributes to it, when stripped of the circumstances of place and time, characteristics which it does not really possess; and this takes place especially in the case of the phenomena of the past, and the more fully in the measure of their antiquity. From these two principles the Modernists deduce two laws, which, when united with a third which they have already derived from agnosticism, constitute the foundation of historic criticism. An example may be sought in the Person of Christ. In the Person of Christ, they say, science and history encounter nothing that is not human. Therefore, in virtue of the first canon deduced from agnosticism, whatever there is in His history suggestive of the divine, must be rejected. Then, according to the second canon, the historical Person of Christ was *transfigured* by faith; therefore everything that raises it above historical conditions must be removed. Lastly, the third canon, which lays down that the Person of Christ has been *disfigured* by faith, requires that everything should be excluded, deeds and words and all else, that is not in strict keeping with His character, condition, and education, and with the place and time in which He lived. A method of reasoning which is passing strange, but in it we have the Modernist criticism.

It is thus that the *religious sense*, which through the agency of *vital immanence* emerges from the lurking-places of the *subconsciousness*, is the germ of all religion, and the explanation of everything that has been or ever will be in any religion. This *sense*, which was at first only rudimentary and almost formless, under the influence of that mysterious principle from which it originated, gradually matured with the progress of human life, of which, as has been said, it is a certain form. This, then, is the origin of all, even of supernatural religion. For religions are mere developments of this *religious sense*. Nor is the Catholic religion an exception; it is quite on a level with the rest; for it was engendered, by the process of *vital immanence*, and by no other way, in the consciousness of Christ, who was a man of the choicest nature, whose like has never been, nor will be. In hearing these things we shudder indeed at so great an audacity of assertion and so great a sacrilege. And yet, Venerable Brethren, these are not merely the foolish babblings of unbelievers. There are Catholics, yea, and priests too, who say these things openly; and they boast that they are going to reform the Church by these ravings! The question is no longer one of the old error which claimed for human nature a sort of right to the supernatural. It has gone far beyond that, and has reached the point when it is affirmed that our most holy religion, in the man Christ as in us, emanated from nature spontaneously and of itself. Nothing assuredly could be more utterly destructive of the whole supernatural order. For this reason the Vatican Council most justly decreed: "If anyone says that man cannot be raised by God to a knowledge and perfection which surpasses nature, but that he can and should, by his own efforts and by a constant development, attain finally to the possession of all truth and good, let him be anathema." *

### [THE ORIGIN OF DOGMAS]

So far, Venerable Brethren, there has been no

* *De Revel.*, can. 3.

mention of the intellect. It also, according to the teaching of the Modernists, has its part in the act of faith. And it is of importance to see how. In that *sense* of which We have frequently spoken, since *sense* is not knowledge, they say God, indeed, presents Himself to man, but in a manner so confused and indistinct that He can hardly be perceived by the believer. It is therefore necessary that a certain light should be cast upon this sense so that God may clearly stand out in relief and be set apart from it. This is the task of the intellect, whose office it is to reflect and to analyse; and by means of it, man first transforms into mental pictures the vital phenomena which arise within him, and then expresses them in words. Hence the common saying of Modernists: that the religious man must *think* his faith. The mind then, encountering this *sense*, throws itself upon it, and works in it after the manner of a painter who restores to greater clearness the lines of a picture that have been dimmed with age. The simile is that of one of the leaders of Modernism. The operation of the mind in this work is a double one: first, by a natural and spontaneous act it expresses its concept in a simple, popular statement; then, on reflection and deeper consideration, or, as they say, *by elaborating its thought*, it expresses the idea in *secondary* propositions, which are derived from the first, but are more precise and distinct. These *secondary* propositions, if they finally receive the approval of the supreme magisterium of the Church, constitute *dogma.*

We have thus reached one of the principal points in the Modernists' system, namely, the origin and the nature of dogma. For they place the origin of dogma in those primitive and simple formulæ, which, under a certain aspect, are necessary to faith; for revelation, to be truly such, requires the clear knowledge of God in the consciousness. But dogma itself, they apparently hold, strictly consists in the *secondary* formulæ.

To ascertain the nature of dogma, we must first find the relation which exists between the *religious formulas* and the *religious sense.* This will be readily perceived by anyone who holds that these *formulas* have no other purpose than to furnish the believer with a means of giving to himself an account of his faith. These formulas therefore stand midway between the believer and his faith; in their relation to the faith they are the inadequate expression of its object, and are usually called *symbols;* in their relation to the believer they are mere *instruments.*

[ITS EVOLUTION]

Hence it is quite impossible to maintain that they absolutely contain the truth: for, in so far as they are *symbols,* they are the images of truth, and so must be adapted to the religious sense in its relation to man; and as *instruments*, they are the vehicles of truth, and must therefore in their turn be adapted to man in his relation to the religious sense. But the object of the *religious sense*, as something contained in the *absolute*, possesses an infinite variety of aspects, of which now one, now another, may present itself. In like manner he who believes can avail himself of varying conditions. Consequently, the formulæ which we call dogma must be subject to these vicissitudes, and are, therefore, liable to change. Thus the way is open to the intrinsic *evolution* of dogma. Here we have an immense structure of sophisms which ruin and wreck all religion. Dogma is not only able, but ought to evolve and to be changed. This is strongly affirmed by the Modernists, and clearly flows from their principles. For amongst the chief points of their teaching is the following, which they deduce from the principle of *vital immanence*, namely, that *religious formulas*, if they are to be really *religious* and not merely intellectual speculations, ought to be living and to live the life of the *religious sense*. This is not to be understood to mean that these formulas, especially if merely imaginative, were to be invented for the religious sense. Their origin matters nothing, any more than their number or quality. What is necessary is that the *religious sense*—with some modification when needful—should vitally assimilate them. In other words, it is necessary that the *primitive formula* be accepted and sanctioned by the heart; and similarly the subsequent work from which are brought forth the *secondary formulas* must proceed under the guidance of the heart. Hence it comes that these formulas, in order to be living, should be, and should remain, adapted to the faith and to him who believes. Wherefore, if for any reason this adaptation should cease to exist, they lose their first meaning and accordingly need to be changed. In view of the fact that the character and lot of dogmatic formulas are so unstable, it is no wonder that Modernists should regard them so lightly and in such open disrespect, and have no consideration or praise for anything but the religious sense and for the religious life. In this way, with consummate audacity, they criticise the Church, as having strayed from the true path by failing to distinguish between the religious and moral sense of formulas and their surface meaning, and by clinging vainly and tenaciously to meaningless formulas, while religion itself is allowed to go to ruin. "Blind" they are, and "leaders of the blind" puffed up with the proud name of science, they have reached that pitch of folly at which they pervert the eternal concept of truth and the true meaning of religion; in introducing a new system in which "they are seen to be under the sway of a blind and unchecked passion for novelty, thinking not at all of finding some solid foundation of truth, but despising the holy and apostolic traditions, they embrace other and vain, futile, uncertain doctrines, unapproved by the Church, on which, in the height of their vanity, they think they can base and maintain truth itself."*

### [THE MODERNIST AS BELIEVER: INDIVIDUAL EXPERIENCE AND RELIGIOUS CERTITUDE]

Thus far, Venerable Brethren, We have considered the Modernist as a Philosopher. Now if we proceed to consider him as a believer, and seek to know how the believer, according to Modernism, is marked off from the Philosopher, it must be observed that, although the Philosopher recognises the *reality of the divine* as the object of faith, still this *reality* is not to be found by him but in the heart of the believer, as an object of feeling and affirmation, and therefore confined within the sphere of phenomena; but the question as to whether in itself it exists outside that feeling and affirmation is one which the Philosopher passes over and neglects. For the Modernist believer, on the contrary, it is an established and certain fact that the *reality* of the divine does really exist in itself and quite independently of the person who believes in it. If you ask on what foundation this assertion of the believer rests,

* Gregory XVI., Encycl. *Singulari Nos*, 7 Kal. Jul. 1834.

he answers: In the personal *experience* of the individual. On this head the Modernists differ from the Rationalists only to fall into the views of the Protestants and pseudo-Mystics. The following is their manner of stating the question: In *the religious sense* one must recognise a kind of intuition of the heart which puts man in immediate contact with the *reality* of God, and infuses such a persuasion of God's existence and His action both within and without man as far to exceed any scientific conviction. They assert, therefore, the existence of a real experience, and one of a kind that surpasses all rational experience. If this experience is denied by some, like the Rationalists, they say that this arises from the fact that such persons are unwilling to put themselves in the moral state necessary to produce it. It is this *experience* which makes the person who acquires it to be properly and truly a believer.

How far this position is removed from that of Catholic teaching! We have already seen how its fallacies have been condemned by the Vatican Council. Later on, we shall see how these errors, combined with those which we have already mentioned, open wide the way to Atheism. Here it is well to note at once that, given this doctrine of *experience* united with that of *symbolism*, every religion, even that of paganism, must be held to be true. What is to prevent such experiences from being found in any religion? In fact, that they are so is maintained by not a few. On what grounds can Modernists deny the truth of an experience affirmed by a follower of Islam? Will they claim a monopoly of true experiences for Catholics alone? Indeed, Modernists do not deny, but actually maintain, some confusedly, others frankly, that all religions are true. That they cannot feel otherwise is obvious. For on what ground, according to their theories, could falsity be predicted of any religion whatsoever? Certainly it would be either on account of the falsity of the *religious sense* or on account of the falsity of the formula pronounced by the mind. Now the *religious sense*, although it may be more perfect or less perfect, is always one and the same; and the intellectual formula, in order to be true, has but to respond to the *religious sense* and to the believer, whatever be the intellectual capacity of the latter. In the conflict between different religions, the most that Modernists can maintain is that the Catholic has more truth because it is more vivid, and that it deserves with more reason the name of Christian because it corresponds more fully with the origins of Christianity. No one will find it unreasonable that these consequences flow from the premises. But what is most amazing is that there are Catholics and priests, who, We would fain believe, abhor such enormities, and yet act as if they fully approved of them. For they lavish such praise and bestow such public honour on the teachers of these errors as to convey the belief that their admiration is not meant merely for the persons, who are perhaps not devoid of a certain merit, but rather for the sake of the errors which these persons openly profess and which they do all in their power to propagate.

## [RELIGIOUS EXPERIENCE AND TRADITION]

There is yet another element in this part of their teaching which is absolutely contrary to Catholic truth. For what is laid down as to *experience* is also applied with destructive effect to *tradition*, which has always been maintained by the Catholic Church. Tradition, as understood by the Modernists, is a communication with others of an *original experience*, through preaching by means of the intellectual formula. To this formula, in addition to its *representative* value, they attribute a species of *suggestive* efficacy which acts firstly in the believer by stimulating the *religious sense*, should it happen to have grown sluggish, and by renewing the *experience* once acquired, and secondly, in those who do not yet believe by awakening in them for the first time the *religious sense* and producing the *experience*. In this way is religious experience spread abroad among the nations; and not merely among contemporaries by preaching, but among future generations both by books and by oral transmission from one to another. Sometimes this communication of religious experience takes root and thrives, at other times it withers at once and dies. For the Modernists, to live is a proof of truth, since for them life and truth are one and the same thing. Thus we are once more led to infer that all existing religions are equally true, for otherwise they would not survive.

### [FAITH AND SCIENCE]

We have proceeded sufficiently far, Venerable Brethren, to have before us enough, and more than enough, to enable us to see what are the relations which Modernists establish between faith and science—including, as they are wont to do under that name, history. And in the first place it is to be held that the object-matter of the one is quite extraneous to and separate from the object-matter of the other. For faith occupies itself solely with something which science declares to be for it *unknowable*. Hence each has a separate scope assigned to it: science is entirely concerned with phenomena, into which faith does not at all enter; faith, on the contrary, concerns itself with the divine, which is entirely unknown to science. Thus it is contended that there can never be any dissension between faith and science, for if each keeps on its own ground they can never meet and therefore never can be in contradiction. And if it be objected that in the visible world there are some things which appertain to faith, such as the human life of Christ, the Modernists reply by denying this. For though such things come within the category of phenomena, still in as far as they are *lived* by faith and in the way already described have been by faith *transfigured* and *disfigured*, they have been removed from the world of sense and transferred into material for the divine. Hence should it be further asked whether Christ has wrought real miracles, and made real prophecies, whether He rose truly from the dead and ascended into Heaven, the answer of agnostic science will be in the negative and the answer of faith in the affirmative—yet there will not be, on that account, any conflict between them. For it will be denied by the philosopher as a philosopher speaking to philosophers and considering Christ only in His *historical reality;* and it will be affirmed by the believer as a believer speaking to believers and considering the life of Christ as *lived again* by the faith and in the faith.

### [FAITH SUBJECT TO SCIENCE]

It would be a great mistake, nevertheless, to suppose that, according to these theories, one is allowed to believe that faith and science are entirely independent of each other. On the side of science that is indeed quite true and correct, but it is quite otherwise with regard to faith, which is subject to science, not on one but on three grounds. For in the first place it must be observed that in every religious fact, when one takes away the *divine reality* and the *experience* of it which the believer possesses, everything else, and especially the *religious formulas*, belongs to the sphere of phenomena and therefore falls under the control of science. Let the believer go out of the world if he will, but so long as he remains in it, whether he like it or not, he cannot escape from the laws, the observation, the judgments of science and of history. Further, although it is contended that God is the object of faith alone, the statement refers only to the *divine reality*, not to the *idea* of God. The latter also is subject to science which, while it philosophises in what is called the logical order, soars also to the absolute and the ideal. It is therefore the right of philosophy and of science to form its knowledge concerning the idea of God, to direct it in its evolution and to purify it of any extraneous elements which may have entered into it. Hence we have the Modernist axiom that the religious evolution ought to be brought into accord with the moral and intellectual, or as one whom they regard as their leader has expressed it, ought to be subject to it. Finally, man does not suffer a dualism to exist in himself, and the believer therefore feels within him an impelling need so to harmonise faith with science that it may never oppose the general conception which science sets forth concerning the universe.

Thus it is evident that science is to be entirely independent of faith, while on the other hand, and notwithstanding that they are supposed to be strangers to each other, faith is made subject to science. All this, Venerable Brothers, is in formal opposition to the teachings of Our Predecessor, Pius IX., where he lays it down that: "In matters of religion it is the duty of philosophy not to command but to serve, not to prescribe what is to be believed, but to embrace what is to be believed with reasonable obedience, not to scrutinise the depths of the mysteries of God, but to venerate them devoutly and humbly." *

The Modernists completely invert the parts, and to them may be applied the words which another of Our Predecessors, Gregory IX., addressed to some theologians of his time: "Some among you, puffed up like bladders with the spirit of vanity, strive by profane novelties to cross the boundaries fixed by the Fathers, twisting the meaning of the sacred text . . . to the philosophical teaching of the rational-

* Brief to the Bishop of Wratislau, June 15th, 1857.

ists, not for the profit of their hearer but to make a show of science . . . these men, led away by various and strange doctrines, turn the head into the tail and force the queen to serve the handmaid." *

[THE METHODS OF MODERNISTS]

This will appear more clearly to anybody who studies the conduct of Modernists, which is in perfect harmony with their teachings. In their writings and addresses they seem not unfrequently to advocate doctrines which are contrary one to the other, so that one would be disposed to regard their attitude as double and doubtful. But this is done deliberately and advisedly, and the reason of it is to be found in their opinion as to the mutual separation of science and faith. Thus in their books one finds some things which might well be approved by a Catholic, but on turning over the page one is confronted by other things which might well have been dictated by a rationalist. When they write history they make no mention of the divinity of Christ, but when they are in the pulpit they profess it clearly; again, when they are dealing with history they take no account of the Fathers and the Councils, but when they catechise the people, they cite them respectfully. In the same way they draw their distinctions between exegesis which is theological and

* Ep. ad Magistros theol. Paris, non Jul. 1223 [*sic*].

pastoral and exegesis which is scientific and historical. So, too, when they treat of philosophy, history, and criticism, acting on the principle that science in no way depends upon faith, they feel no especial horror in treading in the footsteps of Luther * and are wont to display a manifold contempt for Catholic doctrines, for the Holy Fathers, for the Œcumenical Councils, for the Ecclesiastical Magisterium; and should they be taken to task for this, they complain that they are being deprived of their liberty. Lastly, maintaining the theory that faith must be subject to science, they continuously and openly rebuke the Church on the ground that she resolutely refuses to submit and accommodate her dogmas to the opinions of philosophy; while they, on their side, having for this purpose blotted out the old theology, endeavour to introduce a new theology which shall support the aberrations of philosophers.

### [THE MODERNIST AS THEOLOGIAN: HIS PRINCIPLES, IMMANENCE AND SYMBOLISM]

At this point, Venerable Brethren, the way is opened for us to consider the Modernists in the theological arena—a difficult task, yet one that may be disposed of briefly. It is a question of effecting

* Prop. 29 damn. a Leone X. Bull, *Exsurge Domine* 16 maii, 1520. *Via nobis facta est enervandi auctoritatem Conciliorum, et libere contradicendi eorum gestis, et iudicandi eorum decreta, et confidenter confitendi quidquid verum videtur, sive probatum fuerit, sive reprobatum a quocumque Concilio.*

the conciliation of faith with science, but always by making the one subject to the other. In this matter the Modernist theologian takes exactly the same principles which we have seen employed by the Modernist philosopher—the principles of *immanence* and *symbolism*—and applies them to the believer. The process is an extremely simple one. The philosopher has declared: *The principle of faith is immanent;* the believer has added: *This principle is God;* and the theologian draws the conclusion: *God is immanent in man.* Thus we have *theological immanence.* So, too, the philosopher regards it as certain that *the representations of the object of faith are merely symbolical;* the believer has likewise affirmed that *the object of faith is God in himself;* and the theologian proceeds to affirm that: *The representations of the divine reality are symbolical.* And thus we have *theological symbolism.* These errors are truly of the gravest kind and the pernicious character of both will be seen clearly from an examination of their consequences. For, to begin with *symbolism,* since symbols are but symbols in regard to their objects and only instruments in regard to the believer, it is necessary first of all, according to the teachings of the Modernists, that the believer do not lay too much stress on the formula, as formula, but avail himself of it only for the purpose of uniting himself to the absolute truth which the formula at once reveals and conceals, that is to say, endeavours to express but without ever succeeding in doing so. They would also have the believer make use of the formulas only in as far as they are helpful to him, for they are given to be a help and not a hindrance; with proper regard, however, for the social respect due to formulas which the public magisterium has deemed suitable for expressing the common consciousness until such time as the same magisterium shall provide otherwise. Concerning *immanence* it is not easy to determine what Modernists precisely mean by it, for their own opinions on the subject vary. Some understand it in the sense that God working in man is more intimately present in him than man is even in himself; and this conception, if properly understood, is irreproachable. Others hold that the divine action is one with the action of nature, as the action of the first cause is one with the action of the secondary cause; and this would destroy the supernatural order. Others, finally, explain it in a way which savours of pantheism, and this, in truth, is the sense which best fits in with the rest of their doctrines.

With this principle of *immanence* is connected another which may be called the principle of *divine permanence*. It differs from the first in much the same way as the private *experience* differs from the *experience* transmitted by tradition. An example illustrating what is meant will be found in the Church and the Sacraments. The Church and the Sacraments, according to the Modernists, are not to be regarded as having been instituted by Christ Himself. This is barred by agnosticism, which recognises in Christ nothing more than a man whose religious consciousness has been, like that of all men, formed by degrees; it is also barred by the law of immanence, which rejects what they call external *application*; it is further barred by the law of evolution, which requires for the development of the germs, time and a certain series of circumstances; it is, finally, barred by history, which shows that such in fact has been the course of things. Still it is to be held that both Church and Sacraments have been founded *mediately* by Christ. But how? In this way: All Christian consciences were, they affirm, in a manner virtually included in the conscience of Christ as the plant is included in the seed. But as the branches live the life of the seed, so, too, all Christians are to be said to live the life of Christ. But the life of Christ, according to faith, is divine, and so, too, is the life of Christians. And if this life produced, in the course of ages, both the Church and the Sacraments, it is quite right to say that their origin is from Christ and is divine. In the same way they make out that the Holy Scriptures and the dogmas are divine. And in this, the Modernist theology may be said to reach its completion. A slender provision, in truth, but more than enough for the theologian who professes that the conclusions of science, whatever they may be, must always be accepted! No one will have any difficulty in making the application of these theories to the other points with which We propose to deal.

### [DOGMA AND THE SACRAMENTS]

Thus far We have touched upon the origin and nature of faith. But as faith has many branches, and chief among them the Church, dogma, worship, devotions, the Books which we call "Sacred," it concerns us to know what do the Modernists teach concerning them. To begin with dogma, We have already indicated its origin and nature. Dogma is born of a sort of impulse or necessity by virtue of which the believer elaborates his thought so as to render it clearer to his own conscience and that of others. This elaboration consists entirely in the process of investigating and refining the primitive mental *formula*, not indeed in itself and according to any logical explanation, but according to circumstances, or *vitally* as the Modernists somewhat less intelligibly describe it. Hence it happens that around this *primitive* formula *secondary* formulas, as we have already indicated, gradually continue to be formed, and these subsequently grouped into one body, or one doctrinal construction, and further sanctioned by the public magisterium as responding to the common consciousness, are called dogma. Dogma is to be carefully distinguished from the speculations of theologians which, although not alive with the life of dogma, are not without their utility as serving both to harmonise religion with science and to remove opposition between them, and to illumine and defend religion from without, and it may be even to prepare the matter for future dogma. Concerning worship there would not be much to be said, were it not that under this head are comprised the Sacraments, concerning which the Modernist errors are of the most serious character. For them the Sacraments are the resultant of a double impulse or need—for, as we have seen, everything in their system is explained by inner impulses or necessities. The first need is that of giving some sensible manifestation to religion; the second is that of expressing it, which could not be done without some sensible form and consecrating acts, and these are called Sacraments. But for the Modernists, Sacraments are bare symbols or signs, though not devoid of a certain efficacy—an efficacy, they tell us, like that of certain phrases vulgarly described as having caught the popular ear, inasmuch as they have the power of putting certain leading ideas into circulation, and of making a marked impression upon the mind. What the phrases are to the ideas, that the Sacraments are to the religious sense, that and nothing more. The Modernists would express their mind more clearly were they to affirm that the Sacraments are instituted solely to foster the faith—but this is condemned by the Council of Trent: *If anyone say that these Sacraments are instituted solely to foster the faith, let him be anathema.* *

[THE HOLY SCRIPTURES]

We have already touched upon the nature and origin of the Sacred Books. According to the principles of the Modernists they may be rightly described as a summary of *experiences*, not indeed of the kind that may now and again come to anybody, but those extraordinary and striking experiences which are the possession of every religion. And this is precisely what they teach about our books of the Old and New Testament. But to suit their own theories they note with remarkable ingenuity that, although experience is something belonging to the present, still it may draw its material in like manner from the past and the future, inasmuch as the believer by memory *lives* the past over again after the manner *of the present*, and lives the future already by anticipation. This explains how it is that the historical and apocalyptic books are included among the

* *Sess. VII. de Sacramentis in genere, can.* 5.

Sacred Writings. God does indeed speak in these books through the medium of the believer, but according to Modernist theology, only by *immanence* and *vital permanence*. We may ask, what then becomes of inspiration? Inspiration, they reply, is in nowise distinguished from that impulse which stimulates the believer to reveal the faith that is in him by words or writing, except perhaps by its vehemence. It is something like that which happens in poetical inspiration, of which it has been said: There is a God in us, and when He stirreth He sets us afire. It is in this sense that God is said to be the origin of the inspiration of the Sacred Books. The Modernists moreover affirm concerning this inspiration, that there is nothing in the Sacred Books which is devoid of it. In this respect some might be disposed to consider them as more orthodox than certain writers in recent times who somewhat restrict inspiration, as, for instance, in what has been put forward as so-called *tacit citations*. But in all this we have mere verbal conjuring. For if we take the Bible, according to the standards of agnosticism, namely, as a human work, made by men for men, albeit the theologian is allowed to proclaim that it is divine by *immanence*, what room is there left in it for inspiration? The Modernists assert a general inspiration of the Sacred Books, but they admit no inspiration in the Catholic sense.

## [THE CHURCH]

A wider field for comment is opened when we come to what the Modernist school has imagined to be the nature of the Church. They begin with the supposition that the Church has its birth in a double need; first, the need of the individual believer to communicate his faith to others, especially if he has had some original and special experience, and secondly, when the faith has become common to many, the need of the *collectivity* to form itself into a society and to guard, promote, and propagate the common good. What, then, is the Church? It is the product of the *collective conscience*, that is to say of the association of individual consciences which by virtue of the principle of *vital permanence*, depend all on one first believer, who for Catholics is Christ. Now every society needs a directing authority to guide its members towards the common end, to foster prudently the elements of cohesion, which in a religious society are doctrine and worship. Hence the triple authority in the Catholic Church, *disciplinary*, *dogmatic*, *liturgical*. The nature of this authority is to be gathered from its origin, and its rights and duties from its nature. In past times it was a common error that authority came to the Church from without, that is to say, directly from God; and it was then rightly held to be *autocratic*. But this conception has now grown obsolete. For in the same way as the Church is a vital emanation of the collectivity of consciences, so too authority emanates vitally from the Church itself. Authority, therefore, like the Church, has its origin in the religious conscience, and, that being so, is subject to it. Should it disown this dependence it becomes a tyranny. For we are living in an age when the sense of liberty has reached its highest development. In the civil order the public conscience has introduced popular government. Now there is in man only one conscience, just as there is only one life. It is for the ecclesiastical authority, therefore, to adopt a democratic form, unless it wishes to provoke and foment an intestine conflict in the consciences of mankind. The penalty of refusal is disaster. For it is madness to think that the sentiment of liberty, as it now obtains, can recede. Were it forcibly pent up and held in bonds, the more terrible would be its outburst, sweeping away at once both Church and religion. Such is the situation in the minds of the Modernists, and their one great anxiety is, in consequence, to find a way of conciliation between the authority of the Church and the liberty of the believers.

[THE RELATIONS BETWEEN CHURCH AND STATE]

But it is not only within her own household that

the Church must come to terms. Besides her relations with those within, she has others with those who are outside. The Church does not occupy the world all by herself; there are other societies in the world, with which she must necessarily have dealings and contact. The rights and duties of the Church towards civil societies must, therefore, be determined, and determined, of course, by her own nature, that to wit, which the Modernists have already described to us. The rules to be applied in this matter are clearly those which have been laid down for science and faith, though in the latter case the question turned upon the *object*, while in the present case we have one of *ends*. In the same way, then, as faith and science are alien to each other by reason of the diversity of their *objects*, Church and State are strangers by reason of the diversity of their ends, that of the Church being spiritual while that of the State is temporal. Formerly it was possible to subordinate the temporal to the spiritual and to speak of some questions as *mixed*, conceding to the Church the position of queen and mistress in all such, because the Church was then regarded as having been instituted immediately by God as the author of the supernatural order. But this doctrine is to-day repudiated alike by philosophers and historians. The State must, therefore, be separated from the Church, and the Catholic from the citizen.

Every Catholic, from the fact that he is also a citizen, has the right and the duty to work for the common good in the way he thinks best, without troubling himself about the authority of the Church, without paying any heed to its wishes, its counsels, its orders —nay, even in spite of its rebukes. For the Church to trace out and prescribe for the citizen any line of action, on any pretext whatsoever, is to be guilty of an abuse of authority, against which one is bound to protest with all one's might. Venerable Brethren, the principles from which these doctrines spring have been solemnly condemned by Our predecessor, Pius VI., in his Apostolic Constitution *Auctorem fidei.**

[THE MAGISTERIUM OF THE CHURCH]

But it is not enough for the Modernist school that the State should be separated from the Church. For as faith is to be subordinated to science as far as phenomenal elements are concerned, so too in temporal matters the Church must be subject to the State. This, indeed, Modernists may not yet say

* Prop. 2. Propositio, quae statuit, potestatem a Deo datam Ecclesiae ut communicaretur Pastoribus, qui sunt eius ministri pro salute animarum; sic intellecta, ut a communitate fidelium in Pastores derivetur ecclesiastici ministerii ac regiminis potestas: haeretica.—Prop. 3. Insuper, quae statuit Romanum Pontificem esse caput ministeriale; sic explicata ut Romanus Pontifex non a Christo in persona beati Petri, sed ab Ecclesia potestatem ministerii accipiat, qua velut Petri successor, verus Christi vicarius ac totius Ecclesiae caput pollet in universa Ecclesia: haeretica.

openly, but they are forced by the logic of their position to admit it. For granted the principle that in temporal matters the State possesses the sole power, it will follow that when the believer, not satisfied with merely internal acts of religion, proceeds to external acts—such for instance as the reception or administration of the Sacraments—these will fall under the control of the State. What will then become of ecclesiastical authority, which can only be exercised by external acts? Obviously it will be completely under the dominion of the State. It is this inevitable consequence which urges many among *liberal* Protestants to reject all external worship—nay, all external religious fellowship, and leads them to advocate what they call *individual* religion. If the Modernists have not yet openly proceeded so far, they ask the Church in the meanwhile to follow of her own accord in the direction in which they urge her and to adapt herself to the forms of the State. Such are their ideas about *disciplinary* authority. But much more evil and pernicious are their opinions on *doctrinal* and *dogmatic* authority. The following is their conception of the magisterium of the Church: No religious society, they say, can be a real unit unless the religious conscience of its members be one, and also the formula which they adopt. But this double unity requires a kind of common mind whose office is to find and determine the formula that corresponds best with the common conscience; and it must have, moreover, an authority sufficient to enable it to impose on the community the formula which has been decided upon. From the combination and, as it were, fusion of these two elements, the common mind which draws up the formula and the authority which imposes it, arises, according to the Modernists, the notion of the ecclesiastical magisterium. And, as this magisterium springs, in its last analysis, from the individual consciences and possesses its mandate of public utility for their benefit, it necessarily follows that the ecclesiastical magisterium must be dependent upon them, and should therefore be made to bow to the popular ideals. To prevent individual consciences from expressing freely and openly the impulses they feel, to hinder criticism from urging forward dogma in the path of its necessary evolution, is not a legitimate use but an abuse of a power given for the public weal. So too a due method and measure must be observed in the exercise of authority. To condemn and prescribe a work without the knowledge of the author, without hearing his explanations, without discussion, is something approaching to tyranny. And here again it is a question of finding a way of reconciling the full rights of authority on the one hand and those of liberty on the other. In the meantime the proper course for the Catholic will be to proclaim publicly his profound respect for authority, while never ceasing to follow his own judgment. Their general direction for the Church is as follows: That the ecclesiastical authority, since its end is entirely spiritual, should strip itself of that external pomp which adorns it in the eyes of the public. In this, they forget that while religion is for the soul, it is not exclusively for the soul, and that the honour paid to authority is reflected back on Christ who instituted it.

### [THE EVOLUTION OF DOCTRINE]

To conclude this whole question of faith and its various branches, we have still to consider, Venerable Brethren, what the Modernists have to say about the development of the one and the other. First of all they lay down the general principle that in a living religion everything is subject to change, and must in fact be changed. In this way they pass to what is practically their principal doctrine, namely, *evolution*. To the laws of evolution everything is subject under penalty of death—dogma, Church, worship, the Books we revere as sacred, even faith itself. The enunciation of this principle will not be a matter of surprise to anyone who bears in mind what the Modernists have had to say about each of these subjects. Having laid down this law of evolution, the Modernists themselves teach us how it operates. And first, with regard to faith. The primitive form of faith, they tell us, was rudimentary and common to all men alike, for it had its origin in human nature and human life. Vital evolution brought with it progress, not by the accretion of new and purely adventitious forms from without, but by an increasing perfusion of the religious sense into the conscience. The progress was of two kinds: *negative*, by the elimination of all extraneous elements, such, for example, as those derived from the family or nationality; and *positive*, by that intellectual and moral refining of man, by means of which the idea of the divine became fuller and clearer, while the *religious sense* became more acute. For the progress of faith the same causes are to be assigned as those which are adduced above to explain its origin. But to them must be added those extraordinary men whom we call prophets—of whom Christ was the greatest—both because in their lives and their words there was something mysterious which faith attributed to the divinity, and because it fell to their lot to have new and original *experiences* fully in harmony with the religious needs of their time. The progress of dogma is due chiefly to the fact that obstacles to the faith have to be surmounted, enemies have to be vanquished, and objections have to be refuted. Add to this a perpetual striving to penetrate ever more profoundly into those things which are contained in the mysteries of faith. Thus, putting aside other examples, it is found to have happened in the case of Christ: in Him that divine something which faith recognised in Him was slowly and gradually expanded in such a way that He was at last held to be God. The chief stimulus of the evolution of worship consists in the need of accommodation to the manners and customs of peoples, as well as the need of availing itself of the value which certain acts have acquired by usage. Finally, evolution in the Church itself is fed by the need of adapting itself to historical conditions and of harmonising itself with existing forms of society. Such is their view with regard to each. And here, before proceeding further, We wish to draw attention to this whole theory of *necessities or needs*, for beyond all that we have seen, it is, as it were, the base and foundation of that famous method which they describe as historical.

Although evolution is urged on by needs or necessities, yet, if controlled by these alone, it would easily overstep the boundaries of tradition, and thus, separated from its primitive vital principle, would make for ruin instead of progress. Hence, by those who study more closely the ideas of the Modernists, evolution is described as a resultant from the conflict of two forces, one of them tending towards progress, the other towards conservation. The conserving force exists in the Church and is found in tradition; tradition is represented by religious authority, and this both by right and in fact. For by right it is in the very nature of authority to protect tradition, and, in fact, since authority, raised as it is above the contingencies of life, feels hardly, or not at all, the spurs of progress. The progressive force, on the contrary, which responds to the inner needs, lies in the individual consciences and works in them—especially in such of them as are in more close and intimate contact with life. Already we observe, Venerable Brethren, the introduction of that most pernicious doctrine which would make of the laity the factor of progress in the Church. Now it is by a species of covenant and compromise between these two forces of conservatism and progress, that is to say between authority and individual consciences, that changes and advances take place. The individual consciences, or some of them, act on the collective conscience, which brings pressure to bear on the depositaries of authority to make terms and to keep to them.

With all this in mind, one understands how it is that the Modernists express astonishment when they are reprimanded or punished. What is imputed to them as a fault they regard as a sacred duty. They understand the needs of consciences better than anyone else, since they come into closer touch with them than does the ecclesiastical authority. Nay, they embody them, so to speak, in themselves. Hence, for them to speak and to write publicly is a bounden duty. Let authority rebuke them if it pleases—they have their own conscience on their side and an intimate experience which tells them with certainty that what they deserve is not blame but praise. Then they reflect that, after all, there is no progress without a battle and no battle without its victims; and victims they are willing to be like the prophets and Christ Himself. They have no bitterness in their hearts against the authority which uses them roughly, for after all they readily admit that it is only doing its duty as authority. Their sole grief is that it remains deaf to their warnings, for in this way it impedes the progress of souls, but the hour will most surely come when further delay will be impossible, for if the laws of evolution may be checked for a while they cannot be finally evaded. And thus they go their way, reprimands and condemnations notwithstanding, masking an incredible audacity under a mock semblance of humility. While they make a pretence of bowing their heads, their minds and hands are more boldly intent than ever on carrying out their purposes. And this policy they follow willingly and wittingly, both because it is part of their system that authority is to be stimulated but not dethroned, and because it is necessary for them to remain within the ranks of the Church in order that they may gradually transform the collective conscience. And in saying this, they fail to perceive that they are avowing that the collective conscience is not with them, and that they have no right to claim to be its interpreters.

It is thus, Venerable Brethren, that for the Modernists, whether as authors or propagandists, there is to be nothing stable, nothing immutable in the Church. Nor, indeed, are they without forerunners in their doctrines, for it was of these that Our Predecessor Pius IX. wrote: "These enemies of divine revelation extol human progress to the skies, and with rash and sacrilegious daring would have it introduced into the Catholic religion as if this religion were not the work of God but of man, or some kind of philosophical discovery susceptible of perfection by human efforts." * On the subject of revelation and dogma in particular, the doctrine of the Modernists offers nothing new. We find it condemned in the Syllabus of Pius IX., where it is enunciated in these terms: "Divine revelation is imperfect, and therefore subject to continual and indefinite progress, corresponding with the progress of human reason;" † and condemned still more solemnly in the Vatican Council: "The doctrine of

* Encycl. *Qui pluribus*, 9 Nov. 1846. † Syll. Prop. 5.

the faith which God has revealed has not been proposed to human intelligences to be perfected by them as if it were a philosophical system, but as a divine deposit entrusted to the Spouse of Christ to be faithfully guarded and infallibly interpreted. Hence also that sense of the sacred dogmas is to be perpetually retained which our Holy Mother the Church has once declared, nor is this sense ever to be abandoned on plea or pretext of a more profound comprehension of the truth." * Nor is the development of our knowledge, even concerning the faith, barred by this pronouncement; on the contrary, it is supported and maintained. For the same Council continues: "Let intelligence and science and wisdom, therefore, increase and progress abundantly and vigorously in individuals and in the mass, in the believer and in the whole Church, throughout the ages and the centuries—but only in its own kind, that is, according to the same dogma, the same sense, the same acceptation." †

## [THE MODERNIST AS HISTORIAN AND CRITIC]

We have studied the Modernist as philosopher, believer, and theologian. It now remains for us to consider him as historian, critic, apologist, and reformer.

Some Modernists, devoted to historical studies,

* Const. *Dei filius*, cap. iv.

† Loc. cit.

seem to be deeply anxious not to be taken for philosophers. About philosophy they profess to know nothing whatever, and in this they display remarkable astuteness, for they are particularly desirous not to be suspected of any prepossession in favour of philosophical theories which would lay them open to the charge of not being, as they call it, *objective*. And yet the truth is that their history and their criticism are saturated with their philosophy, and that their historico-critical conclusions are the natural outcome of their philosophical principles. This will be patent to anyone who reflects. Their three first laws are contained in those three principles of their philosophy already dealt with; the principle of *agnosticism*, the theorem of the *transfiguration* of things by faith, and that other which may be called the principle of *disfiguration*. Let us see what consequences flow from each of these. *Agnosticism* tells us that history, like science, deals entirely with phenomena, and the consequence is that God, and every intervention of God in human affairs, is to be relegated to the domain of faith as belonging to it alone. Wherefore in things where there is combined a double element, the divine and the human, as, for example, in Christ, or the Church, or the Sacraments, or the many other objects of the same kind, a division and separation must be made and the human element must be left to history while the divine will be assigned to faith. Hence we have that distinction, so current among the Modernists, between the Christ of history and the Christ of faith; the Church of history and the Church of faith; the Sacraments of history and the Sacraments of faith, and so in similar matters. Next we find that the human element itself, which the historian has to work on, as it appears in the documents, is to be considered as having been transfigured by faith, that is to say, raised above its historical conditions. It becomes necessary, therefore, to eliminate also the accretions which faith has added, to relegate them to faith itself and to the history of faith. Thus, when treating of Christ, the historian must set aside all that surpasses man in his natural condition, according to what psychology tells us of him, or according to what we gather from the place and period of his existence. Finally, they require, by virtue of the third principle, that even those things which are not outside the sphere of history, should pass through the sieve, excluding all and relegating to faith everything which, in their judgment, is not in harmony with what they call the *logic* of facts or not in character with the persons of whom they are predicated. Thus, they will not allow that Christ ever uttered those things which do not seem to be within the capacity of the multitudes that listened to Him. Hence they delete from His *real* history and transfer to faith all the allegories found in His discourses. We may peradventure inquire on what principle they make these divisions? Their reply is that they argue from the character of the man, from his condition of life, from his education, from the complexus of the circumstances under which the facts took place, in short, if We understand them aright, on a principle which in the last analysis is merely *subjective.* Their method is to put themselves into the position and person of Christ, and then to attribute to Him what they would have done under like circumstances. In this way, absolutely *a priori* and acting on philosophical principles which they hold but which they profess to ignore, they proclaim that Christ, according to what they call His *real* history, was not God and never did anything divine, and that as man He did and said only what they, judging from the time in which He lived, consider that He ought to have said or done.

### [CRITICISM AND ITS PRINCIPLES]

As history takes its conclusions from philosophy, so too criticism takes its conclusions from history. The critic, on the data furnished him by the historian, makes two parts of all his documents. Those that remain after the triple elimination above described go to form the *real* history; the rest is attributed to the history of the faith or, as it is styled, to *internal* history. For the Modernists distinguish very carefully between these two kinds of history, and it is to be noted that they oppose the history of the faith to *real* history precisely as real. Thus, as we have already said, we have a twofold Christ: a real Christ, and a Christ, the one of faith, who never really existed; a Christ who has lived at a given time and in a given place, and a Christ who has never lived outside the pious meditations of the believer—the Christ, for instance, whom we find in the Gospel of S. John, which, according to them, is mere meditation from beginning to end.

But the dominion of philosophy over history does not end here. Given that division, of which We have spoken, of the documents into two parts, the philosopher steps in again with his dogma of *vital immanence*, and shows how everything in the history of the Church is to be explained by *vital emanation*. And since the cause or condition of every vital emanation whatsoever is to be found in some need or want, it follows that no fact can be regarded as antecedent to the need which produced it—historically the fact must be posterior to the need. What, then, does the historian in view of this principle? He goes over his documents again, whether they be contained in the Sacred Books or elsewhere, draws up from them his list of the particular needs of the Church, whether relating to dogma, or liturgy, or other matters which are found in the Church thus related, and then he hands his list over to the critic. The critic takes in hand the documents dealing with the history of faith and distributes them, period by period, so that they correspond exactly with the list of needs, always guided by the principle that the narration must follow the facts, as the facts follow the needs. It may at times happen that some parts of the Sacred Scriptures, such as the Epistles, themselves constitute the fact created by the need. Even so, the rule holds that the age of any document can only be determined by the age in which each need has manifested itself in the Church. Further, a distinction must be made between the beginning of a fact and its development, for what is born in one day requires time for growth. Hence the critic must once more go over his documents, ranged as they are through the different ages, and divide them again into two parts, separating those that regard the origin of the facts from those that deal with their development, and these he must again arrange according to their periods.

Then the philosopher must come in again to enjoin upon the historian the obligation of following in all his studies the precepts and laws of evolution. It is next for the historian to scrutinise his documents once more, to examine carefully the circumstances and conditions affecting the Church during the different periods, the conserving force she has put forth, the needs both internal and external that have stimulated her to progress, the obstacles she has had to encounter, in a word, everything that helps to determine the manner in which the laws of evolution have been fulfilled in her. This done, he finishes his work by drawing up a history of the development in its broad lines. The critic follows and fits in the rest of the documents. He sets himself to write. The history is finished. Now We ask here: Who is the author of this history? The historian? The critic? Assuredly neither of these but the philosopher. From beginning to end everything in it is *a priori*, and an apriorism that reeks of heresy. These men are certainly to be pitied, of whom the Apostle might well say: *They became vain in their thoughts . . . professing themselves to be wise they became fools* (Rom. i, 21, 22). At the same time, they excite resentment when they accuse the Church of arranging and confusing the texts after her own fashion, and for the needs of her cause. In this they are accusing the Church of something for which their own conscience plainly reproaches them.

### [HOW THE BIBLE IS DEALT WITH]

The result of this dismembering of the records, and this partition of them throughout the centuries, is naturally that the Scriptures can no longer be attributed to the authors whose names they bear. The Modernists have no hesitation in affirming generally that these books, and especially the Pentateuch and the first three Gospels, have been gradually formed from a primitive brief narration, by additions, by interpolations of theological or allegorical interpretations, or parts introduced only for the purpose of joining different passages together. This means, to put it briefly and clearly, that in the Sacred Books we must admit a *vital evolution*, springing from and corresponding with the evolution of faith. The traces of this evolution, they tell us, are so visible in the books that one might almost write a history of it. Indeed, this history they actually do write, and with such an easy assurance that one might believe them to have seen with their own eyes the writers at work through the ages amplifying the Sacred Books. To aid them in this they call to their assistance that branch of criticism which they call *textual*, and labour to show that such a fact or such a phase is not in its right place, adducing other arguments of the same kind. They seem, in fact, to have constructed for themselves certain types of narration and discourses, upon which they base their assured verdict as to whether a thing is or is not out of place. Let him who can judge how far they are qualified in this way to make such distinctions. To hear them descant of their works on the Sacred Books, in which they have been able to discover so much that is defective, one would imagine that before them nobody ever even turned over the pages of Scripture. The truth is that a whole multitude of Doctors, far superior to them in genius, in erudition, in sanctity, have sifted the Sacred Books in every way, and so far from finding in them anything blameworthy have thanked God more and more heartily the more deeply they have gone into them, for His divine bounty in having vouchsafed to speak thus to men. Unfortunately, these great Doctors did not enjoy the same aids to study that are possessed by the Modernists for they did not have for their rule and guide a philosophy borrowed from the negation of God, and a criterion which consists of themselves.

We believe, then, that We have set forth with sufficient clearness the historical method of the Modernists. The philosopher leads the way, the historian follows, and then in due order come the internal and textual critics. And since it is characteristic of the primary cause to communicate its virtue to causes which are secondary, it is quite clear that the criticism with which we are concerned is not any kind of criticism, but that which is rightly called *agnostic, immanentist, and evolutionist* criticism. Hence anyone who adopts it and employs it, makes profession thereby of the errors contained in it, and places himself in opposition to Catholic teaching.

This being so, it is much a matter for surprise that it should have found acceptance to such an extent amongst certain Catholics. Two causes may be assigned for this: first, the close alliance which the historians and critics of this school have formed among themselves independent of all differences of nationality or religion; second, their boundless effrontery by which, if one then makes any utterance, the others applaud him in chorus, proclaiming that science has made another step forward, while if an outsider should desire to inspect the new discovery for himself, they form a coalition against him. He who denies it is decried as one who is ignorant, while he who embraces and defends it has all their praise. In this way they entrap not a few, who, did they but realise what they are doing, would shrink back with horror. The domineering overbearance of those who teach the errors, and the thoughtless compliance of the more shallow minds who assent to them, create a corrupted atmosphere which penetrates everywhere, and carries infection with it. But let Us pass to the apologist.

[THE MODERNIST AS APOLOGIST]

The Modernist apologist depends in two ways on the philosopher. First, *indirectly*, inasmuch as his subject-matter is history—history dictated, as we have seen, by the philosopher; and, secondly, *di-*

*rectly*, inasmuch as he takes both his doctrines and his conclusions from the philosopher. Hence that common axiom of the Modernist school that in the new apologetics controversies in religion must be determined by psychological and historical research. The Modernist apologists, then, enter the arena, proclaiming to the rationalists that, though they are defending religion, they have no intention of employing the data of the Sacred Books or the histories in current use in the Church, and written upon the old lines, but *real* history composed on modern principles and according to the modern method. In all this they assert that they are not using an *argumentum ad hominem*, because they are really of the opinion that the truth is to be found only in this kind of history. They feel that it is not necessary for them to make profession of their own sincerity in their writings. They are already known to and praised by the rationalist as fighting under the same banner, and they not only plume themselves on these encomiums, which would only provoke disgust in a real Catholic, but use them as a counter compensation to the reprimands of the Church.

Let us see how the Modernist conducts his apologetics. The aim he sets before himself is to make one who is still without faith attain that *experience* of the Catholic religion which, according to the system, is the sole basis of faith. There are two ways open to him, the *objective* and the *subjective.* The first of them starts from agnosticism. It tends to show that religion, and especially the Catholic religion is endowed with such vitality as to compel every psychologist and historian of good faith to recognise that its history hides some element of the *unknown.* To this end it is necessary to prove that the Catholic religion, as it exists to-day, is that which was founded by Jesus Christ; that is to say, that it is nothing else than the progressive development of the germ which He brought into the world. Hence it is imperative first of all to establish what this germ was, and this the Modernist claims to be able to do by the following formula: Christ announced the coming of the kingdom of God, which was to be realised within a brief lapse of time and of which He was to become the Messiah, the divinely-given founder and ruler. Then it must be shown how this germ, always *immanent* and *permanent* in the Catholic religion, has gone on slowly developing in the course of history, adapting itself successively to the different circumstances through which it has passed, borrowing from them by *vital* assimilation all the doctrinal, cultual, ecclesiastical forms that served its purpose; whilst, on the other hand, it surmounted all obstacles, vanquished all enemies, and survived all assaults and all combats. Anyone who well and duly considers this mass of obstacles, adversaries, attacks, combats, and the vitality and fecundity which the Church has shown throughout them all, must admit that if the laws of evolution are visible in her life they fail to explain the whole of her history — the *unknown* rises forth from it and presents itself before us. Thus do they argue, not perceiving that their determination of the primitive germ is only an *a priori* assumption of agnostic and evolutionist philosophy, and that the germ itself has been gratuitously defined so that it may fit in with their contention.

But while they endeavour by this line of reasoning to prove and plead for the Catholic religion, these new apologists are more than willing to grant and to recognise that there are in it many things which are repulsive. Nay, they admit openly, and with ill-concealed satisfaction, that they have found that even its dogma is not exempt from errors and contradictions. They add also that this is not only excusable but — curiously enough — that it is even right and proper. In the Sacred Books there are many passages referring to science or history where, according to them, manifest errors are to be found. But, they say, the subject of these books is not science or history, but only religion and morals. In them history and science serve only as a species of covering to enable the religious and moral experiences wrapped up in them to penetrate more readily among the masses. The masses understood science and history as they are expressed in these books, and it is clear that the expression of science and history in a more perfect form would have proved not so much a help as a hindrance. Moreover, they add, the Sacred Books being essentially religious, are necessarily quick with life. Now life has its own truth and its own logic—quite different from rational truth and rational logic, belonging as they do to a different order, viz., truth of adaptation and of proportion both with what they call the *medium* in which it lives and with the end for which it lives. Finally, the Modernists, losing all sense of control, go so far as to proclaim as true and legitimate whatever is explained by life.

We, Venerable Brethren, for whom there is but one and only truth, and who hold that the Sacred Books, *written under the inspiration of the Holy Ghost, have God for their author* * declare that this is equivalent to attributing to God Himself the lie of utility or officious lie, and We say with S. Augustine: *In an authority so high, admit but one officious lie, and there will not remain a single passage of those apparently difficult to practise or to believe, which on the same most pernicious rule may not be explained as a lie uttered by the author wilfully and to serve a purpose.* † And thus it will come about, the holy

* Conc. Vat., *De Revel.*, c. 2.

† Epist. 28.

Doctor continues that *everybody will believe and refuse to believe what he likes or dislikes in them*, namely, the Scriptures. But the Modernists pursue their way eagerly. They grant also that certain arguments adduced in the Sacred Books in proof of a given doctrine, like those, for example, which are based on the prophecies, have no rational foundation to rest on. But they defend even these as artifices of preaching, which are justified by life. More than that. They are ready to admit, nay, to proclaim, that Christ Himself manifestly erred in determining the time when the coming of the kingdom of God was to take place; and they tell us that we must not be surprised at this since even He Himself was subject to the laws of life! After this what is to become of the dogmas of the Church? The dogmas bristle with flagrant contradictions, but what does it matter since, apart from the fact that vital logic accepts them, they are not repugnant to symbolical truth. Are we not dealing with the infinite, and has not the infinite an infinite variety of aspects? In short, to maintain and defend these theories they do not hesitate to declare that the noblest homage that can be paid to the Infinite is to make it the object of contradictory statements! But when they justify even contradictions, what is it that they will refuse to justify?

[SUBJECTIVE ARGUMENTS]

But it is not solely by *objective* arguments that the non-believer may be disposed to faith. There are also those that are *subjective*, and for this purpose the Modernist Apologists return to the doctrine of *immanence*. They endeavour, in fact, to persuade their non-believer that down in the very depths of his nature and his life lie hidden the need and the desire for some religion, and this not a religion of any kind, but the specific religion known as Catholicism, which, they say, is absolutely *postulated* by the perfect development of life. And here again We have grave reason to complain that there are Catholics who, while rejecting *immanence* as a doctrine, employ it as a method of apologetics, and who do this so imprudently that they seem to admit, not merely a capacity and a suitability for the supernatural, such as has at all times been emphasised, within due limits by Catholic apologists, but that there is in human nature a true and rigorous need for the supernatural order. Truth to tell, it is only the moderate Modernists who make this appeal to an exigency for the Catholic religion. As for the others, who might be called *integralists*, they would show to the non-believer, as hidden in his being, the very germ which Christ Himself had in His consciousness, and which He transmitted to mankind.

Such, Venerable Brethren, is a summary description of the apologetic method of the Modernists, in perfect harmony with their doctrines—methods and doctrines replete with errors, made not for edification but for destruction, not for the making of Catholics but for the seduction of those who are Catholics into heresy; and tending to the utter subversion of all religion.

### [THE MODERNIST AS REFORMER]

It remains for Us now to say a few words about the Modernist as reformer. From all that has preceded, it is abundantly clear how great and how eager is the passion of such men for innovation. In all Catholicism there is absolutely nothing on which it does not fasten. They wish philosophy to be reformed, especially in the ecclesiastical seminaries. They wish the scholastic philosophy to be relegated to the history of philosophy and to be classed among obsolete systems, and the young men to be taught modern philosophy which alone is true and suited to the times in which we live. They desire the reform of theology: rational theology is to have modern philosophy for its foundation, and positive theology is to be founded on the history of dogma. As for history, it must be written and taught only according to their methods and modern principles. Dogmas and their evolution, they affirm, are to be harmonised with science and history. In the Catechism no dogmas are to be inserted except those that have been reformed and are within the capacity of the people. Regarding worship, they say, the number of external devotions is to be reduced, and steps must be taken to prevent their further increase, though, indeed, some of the admirers of symbolism are disposed to be more indulgent on this head. They cry out that ecclesiastical government requires to be reformed in all its branches, but especially in its disciplinary and dogmatic departments. They insist that both outwardly and inwardly it must be brought into harmony with the modern conscience, which now wholly tends towards democracy; a share in ecclesiastical government should therefore be given to the lower ranks of the clergy, and even to the laity, and authority which is too much concentrated, should be decentralised. The Roman Congregations, and especially the *Index* and the *Holy Office*, must be likewise modified. The ecclesiastical authority must alter its line of conduct in the social and political world; while keeping outside political organisations, it must adapt itself to them, in order to penetrate them with its spirit. With regard to morals, they adopt the principle of the Americanists, that the active virtues are more important than the passive, and are to be more encouraged in practice. They ask that the clergy should return to their primitive humility and poverty, and that in their ideas and action they should admit the principles of Modernism; and there are some who, gladly listening to the teaching of their Protestant masters, would desire the suppression of the celibacy of the clergy. What is there left in the Church which is not to be reformed by them and according to their principles?

### [MODERNISM THE SYNTHESIS OF ALL THE HERESIES]

It may, perhaps, seem to some, Venerable Brethren, that We have dwelt at too great length on this exposition of the doctrines of the Modernists. But it was necessary that We should do so, both in order to meet their customary charge that We do not understand their ideas, and to show that their system does not consist in scattered and unconnected theories, but, as it were, in a closely connected whole, so that it is not possible to admit one without admitting all. For this reason, too, We have had to give to this exposition a somewhat didactic form, and not to shrink from employing certain unwonted terms which the Modernists have brought into use. And now with Our eyes fixed upon the whole system, no one will be surprised that We should define it to be the synthesis of all heresies? Undoubtedly, were anyone to attempt the task of collecting together all the errors that have been broached against the faith and to concentrate into one the sap and substance of them all, he could not succeed in doing so better than the Modernists have done. Nay, they have gone farther than this, for, as We have already intimated, their system means the destruction not of the Catholic religion alone, but of all religion. Hence the rationalists are not wanting in their applause, and the most frank and sincere amongst them congratulate themselves in having found in the Modernists the most valuable of all allies.

Let us turn for a moment, Venerable Brethren, to that most disastrous doctrine of *agnosticism.* By it every avenue to God on the side of the intellect is barred to man, while a better way is supposed to be opened from the side of a certain sense of the soul and action. But who does not see how mistaken is such a contention? For the sense of the soul is the response to the action of the thing which the intellect or the outward senses set before it. Take away the intelligence, and man, already inclined to follow the senses, becomes their slave. Doubly mistaken, from another point of view, for all these fantasies of the religious sense will never be able to destroy common sense, and common sense tells us that emotion and everything that leads the heart captive proves a hindrance instead of a help to the discovery of truth. We speak of truth in itself—for that other purely *subjective* truth the fruit of the internal sense and action, if it serves its purpose for the play of words, is of no benefit to the man who wants above all things to know whether outside himself there is a God into whose hands he is one day to fall. True, the Modernists call in *experience* to eke out their system, but what does this *experience* add to that sense of the soul? Absolutely nothing beyond a certain intensity and a proportionate deepening of the conviction of the reality of the object. But these two will never make the sense of the soul into anything but sense, nor will they alter its nature, which is liable to deception when the intelligence is not there to guide it; on the contrary, they but confirm and strengthen this nature, for the more intense the sense is the more it is really sense. And as we are here dealing with religious sense and the experience involved in it, it is known to you, Venerable Brethren, how necessary in such a matter is prudence, and the learning by which prudence is guided. You know it from your own dealings with souls, and especially with souls in whom sentiment predominates; you know it also from your reading of works of ascetical theology—works for which the Modernists have but little esteem, but which testify to a science and a solidity far greater than theirs, and to a refinement and subtlety of observation far beyond any which the Modernists take credit to themselves for possessing. It seems to Us nothing short of madness, or at the least consummate temerity, to accept for true, and without investigation, these incomplete experiences which are the vaunt of the Modernist. Let us for a moment put the question: If experiences have so much force and value in their estimation, why do they not attach equal weight to the experience that so many thousands of Catholics have that the Modernists are on the wrong path? Is it that the Catholic experiences are the only ones which are false and deceptive? The vast majority of mankind holds and always will hold firmly that sense and experience alone, when not enlightened and guided by reason, cannot reach to the knowledge of God. What, then, remains but atheism and the absence of all religion. Certainly it is not the doctrine of *symbolism* that will save us from this. For if all the intellectual elements, as they call them, of religion are nothing more than mere symbols of God, will not the very name of God or of divine personality be also a symbol, and if this be admitted, the personality of God will become a matter of doubt and the gate will be opened to Pantheism? And to Pantheism pure and simple that other doctrine of the *divine immanence* leads directly. For this is the question which We ask: Does or does not this *immanence* leave God distinct from man? If it does, in what does it differ from the Catholic doctrine, and why does it reject the doctrine of external revelation? If it does not, it is Pantheism. Now the doctrine of *immanence* in the Modernist acceptation holds and professes that every phenomenon of conscience proceeds from man as man. The rigorous conclusion from this is the identity of man with God, which means Pantheism. The distinction which Modernists make between science and faith leads to the same conclusion. The object of science, they say, is the reality of the knowable; the object of faith, on the contrary, is the reality of the unknowable. Now, what makes the unknowable unknowable is the fact that there is no proportion between its object and the intellect—a defect of proportion which nothing whatever, even in the doctrine of the Modernist, can suppress. Hence the unknowable remains and will eternally remain unknowable to the believer as well as to the philosopher. Therefore if any religion at all is possible, it can only be the religion of an unknowable reality. And why this religion might not be that soul of the universe, of which certain rationalists speak, is something which certainly does not seem to Us apparent. These reasons suffice to show superabundantly by how many roads Modernism leads to atheism and to the annihilation of all religion. The error of Protestantism made the first step on this path; that of Modernism makes the second; Atheism makes the next.

## [PART II.—THE CAUSE OF MODERNISM]

To penetrate still deeper into the meaning of Modernism and to find a suitable remedy for so deep a sore, it behoves Us, Venerable Brethren, to investigate the causes which have engendered it and which foster its growth. That the proximate and immediate cause consists in an error of the mind cannot be open to doubt. We recognise that the remote causes may be reduced to two: curiosity and pride. Curiosity by itself, if not prudently regulated, suffices to account for all errors. Such is the opinion of Our Predecessor, Gregory XVI., who wrote: *A lamentable spectacle is that presented by the aberrations of human reason when it yields to the spirit of novelty, when against the warning of the Apostle it seeks to know beyond what it is meant to know, and when relying too much on itself it thinks it can find the truth outside the Catholic Church wherein truth is found without the slightest shadow of error.**

But it is pride which exercises an incomparably greater sway over the soul to blind it and lead it into error, and pride sits in Modernism as in its own house, finding sustenance everywhere in its doctrines

* Ep. Encycl. *Singulari Nos*, 7 Kal. Jul. 1834.

and lurking in its every aspect. It is pride which fills Modernists with that self-assurance by which they consider themselves and pose as the rule for all. It is pride which puffs them up with that vain-glory which allows them to regard themselves as the sole possessors of knowledge, and makes them say, elated and inflated with presumption, *We are not as the rest of men*, and which, lest they should seem as other men, leads them to embrace and to devise novelties even of the most absurd kind. It is pride which rouses in them the spirit of disobedience and causes them to demand a compromise between authority and liberty. It is owing to their pride that they seek to be the reformers of others while they forget to reform themselves, and that they are found to be utterly wanting in respect for authority, even for the supreme authority. Truly there is no road which leads so directly and so quickly to Modernism as pride. When a Catholic layman or a priest forgets the precept of the Christian life which obliges us to renounce ourselves if we would follow Christ and neglects to tear pride from his heart, then it is he who most of all is a fully ripe subject for the errors of Modernism. For this reason, Venerable Brethren, it will be your first duty to resist such victims of pride, to employ them only in the lowest and obscurest offices. The higher they try to rise, the lower let them be placed, so that the lowliness of their position may limit their power of causing damage. Examine most carefully your young clerics by yourselves and by the directors of your seminaries, and when you find the spirit of pride amongst them reject them without compunction from the priesthood. Would to God that this had always been done with the vigilance and constancy which were required!

If we pass on from the moral to the intellectual causes of Modernism, the first and the chief which presents itself is ignorance. Yes, these very Modernists who seek to be esteemed as Doctors of the Church, who speak so loftily of modern philosophy and show such contempt for scholasticism, have embraced the one with all its false glamour, precisely because their ignorance of the other has left them without the means of being able to recognise confusion of thought and to refute sophistry. Their whole system, containing as it does errors so many and so great, has been born of the union between faith and false philosophy.

### [METHODS OF PROPAGANDISM]

Would that they had but displayed less zeal and energy in propagating it! But such is their activity and such their unwearying labour on behalf of their cause, that one cannot but be pained to see them waste such energy in endeavouring to ruin the Church when they might have been of such service to her had their efforts been better directed. Their artifices to delude men's minds are of two kinds, the first to remove obstacles from their path, the second to devise and apply actively and patiently every resource that can serve their purpose. They recognise that the three chief difficulties which stand in their way are the scholastic method of philosophy, the authority and Tradition of the Fathers, and the magisterium of the Church, and on these they wage unrelenting war. Against scholastic philosophy and theology they use the weapons of ridicule and contempt. Whether it is ignorance or fear, or both, that inspires this conduct in them, certain it is that the passion for novelty is always united in them with hatred of scholasticism, and there is no surer sign that a man is tending to Modernism than when he begins to show his dislike for the scholastic method. Let the Modernists and their admirers remember the proposition condemned by Pius IX.: *The method and principles which have served the ancient doctors of scholasticism when treating of theology no longer correspond with the exigencies of our time or the progress of science.** They exercise all their ingenuity in an effort to weaken the force and falsify the character of tradition, so as to rob it of all its weight

*Syll. Prop. 13.

and authority. But for Catholics nothing will remove the authority of the second Council of Nicea, where it condemns those *who dare, after the impious fashion of heretics, to deride the ecclesiastical traditions, to invent novelties of some kind . . . or endeavour by malice or craft to overthrow any one of the legitimate traditions of the Catholic Church ;* nor that of the declaration of the fourth Council of Constantinople : *We therefore profess to preserve and guard the rules bequeathed to the Holy Catholic and Apostolic Church, by the Holy and most illustrious Apostles, by the orthodox Councils, both general and local, and by every one of those divine interpreters, the Fathers and Doctors of the Church.* Wherefore the Roman Pontiffs, Pius IV. and Pius IX., ordered the insertion in the profession of faith of the following declaration : *I most firmly admit and embrace the apostolic and ecclesiastical traditions and other observances and constitutions of the Church.*

The Modernists pass judgment on the holy Fathers of the Church even as they do upon tradition. With consummate temerity they assure the public that the Fathers, while personally most worthy of all veneration, were entirely ignorant of history and criticism, for which they are only excusable on account of the time in which they lived. Finally, the Modernists try in every way to diminish and weaken the authority of the ecclesiastical magisterium itself by sacrilegiously falsifying its origin, character, and rights, and by freely repeating the calumnies of its adversaries. To the entire band of Modernists may be applied those words which Our Predecessor sorrowfully wrote: *To bring contempt and odium on the mystic Spouse of Christ, who is the true light, the children of darkness have been wont to cast in her face before the world a stupid calumny, and perverting the meaning and force of things and words, to depict her as the friend of darkness and ignorance, and the enemy of light, science, and progress.** This being so, Venerable Brethren, there is little reason to wonder that the Modernists vent all their bitterness and hatred on Catholics who zealously fight the battles of the Church. There is no species of insult which they do not heap upon them, but their usual course is to charge them with ignorance or obstinacy. When an adversary rises up against them with an erudition and force that render him redoubtable, they seek to make a conspiracy of silence around him to nullify the effects of his attack. The policy towards Catholics is the more invidious in that they belaud with admiration which knows no bounds the writers who range themselves on their side, hailing their works, exuding novelty in every page, with a chorus of applause.

---

* Motu Proprio, *Ut Mysticum*, 14 March, 1891.

For them the scholarship of a writer is in direct proportion to the recklessness of his attacks on antiquity, and of his efforts to undermine tradition and the ecclesiastical magisterium. When one of their number falls under the condemnation of the Church the rest of them, to the disgust of good Catholics, gather round him, loudly and publicly applaud him, and hold him up in veneration as almost a martyr for truth. The young, excited and confused by all this clamour of praise and abuse, some of them afraid of being branded as ignorant, others ambitious to rank among the learned, and both classes goaded internally by curiosity and pride, not unfrequently surrender and give themselves up to Modernism.

And here we have already some of the artifices employed by Modernists to exploit their wares. What efforts do they not make to win new recruits! They seize upon professorships in the seminaries and universities, and gradually make of them chairs of pestilence. In sermons from the pulpit they disseminate their doctrines, although possibly in utterances which are veiled. In congresses they express their teachings more openly. In their social gatherings they introduce them and commend them to others. Under their own names and under pseudonyms they publish numbers of books, newspapers, reviews, and sometimes one and the same writer adopts a variety of pseudonyms to trap the incautious reader into believing in a multitude of Modernist writers. In short, with feverish activity they leave nothing untried in act, speech, and writing. And with what result? We have to deplore the spectacle of many young men, once full of promise and capable of rendering great services to the Church, now gone astray. It is also a subject of grief to Us that many others who, while they certainly do not go so far as the former, have yet been so infected by breathing a poisoned atmosphere, as to think, speak, and write with a degree of laxity which ill becomes a Catholic. They are to be found among the laity, and in the ranks of the clergy, and they are not wanting even in the last place where one might expect to meet them, in religious communities. If they treat of biblical questions, it is upon Modernist principles; if they write history, they carefully, and with ill-concealed satisfaction, drag into the light, on the plea of telling the whole truth, everything that appears to cast a stain upon the Church. Under the sway of certain *a priori* conceptions they destroy as far as they can the pious traditions of the people, and bring into disrespect certain relics highly venerable from their antiquity. They are possessed by the empty desire of having their names upon the lips of the public, and they know they would never succeed in this were they to say only what has always been said by all men.

Meanwhile it may be that they have persuaded themselves that in all this they are really serving God and the Church. In reality they only offend both, less perhaps by their works in themselves than by the spirit in which they write, and by the encouragement they thus give to the aims of the Modernists.

## [PART III.—REMEDIES]

Against this host of grave errors, and its secret and open advance, Our Predecessor, Leo XIII., of happy memory, worked strenuously, both in his words and acts, especially as regards the study of the Bible. But, as we have seen, the Modernists are not easily deterred by such weapons. With an affectation of great submission and respect, they proceeded to twist the words of the Pontiff to their own sense, while they described his action as directed against others than themselves. Thus the evil has gone on increasing from day to day. We, therefore, Venerable Brethren, have decided to suffer no longer delay, and to adopt measures which are more efficacious. We exhort and conjure you to see to it that in this most grave matter no one shall be in a position to say that you have been in the slightest degree wanting in vigilance, zeal, or firmness. And what We ask of you and expect of you, We ask and expect also of all other pastors of souls, of all educators and professors of clerics, and in a very special way of the superiors of religious communities.

[I.—THE STUDY OF SCHOLASTIC PHILOSOPHY]

1. In the first place, with regard to studies, We will and strictly ordain that scholastic philosophy be made the basis of the sacred sciences. It goes without saying that *if anything is met with among the scholastic doctors which may be regarded as something investigated with an excess of subtlety, or taught without sufficient consideration; anything which is not in keeping with the certain results of later times; anything, in short, which is altogether destitute of probability, We have no desire whatever to propose it for the imitation of present generations.** And let it be clearly understood above all things that when We prescribe scholastic philosophy We understand chiefly that which the Angelic Doctor has bequeathed to us, and We, therefore, declare that all the ordinances of Our Predecessor on this subject continue fully in force, and, as far as may be necessary, We do decree anew, and confirm, and order that they shall be strictly observed by all. In seminaries where they have been neglected it will be for the Bishops to exact and require their observance in the future; and let this apply also to the Superiors of

* Leo XIII., Enc. *Aeterni Patris.*

religious orders. Further, We admonish Professors to bear well in mind that they cannot set aside S. Thomas, especially in metaphysical questions, without grave disadvantage.

On this philosophical foundation the theological edifice is to be carefully raised. Promote the study of theology, Venerable Brethren, by all means in your power, so that your clerics on leaving the seminaries may carry with them a deep admiration and love of it, and always find in it a source of delight. For *in the vast and varied abundance of studies opening before the mind desirous of truth, it is known to everyone that theology occupies such a commanding place, that according to an ancient adage of the wise, it is the duty of the other arts and sciences to serve it, and to wait upon it after the manner of handmaidens.** We will add that We deem worthy of praise those who with full respect for tradition, the Fathers, and the ecclesiastical magisterium, endeavour, with well-balanced judgment, and guided by Catholic principles (which is not always the case), to illustrate positive theology by throwing upon it the light of true history. It is certainly necessary that positive theology should be held in greater appreciation than it has been in the past, but this must be done without detriment to scholastic theology; and those are to be disapproved as Modern-

* Leo XIII., Lett. ap. *In Magna*, Dec. 10, 1889.

ists who exalt positive theology in such a way as to seem to despise the scholastic.

With regard to secular studies, let it suffice to recall here what Our Predecessor has admirably said: *Apply yourselves energetically to the study of natural sciences: in which department the things that have been so brilliantly discovered, and so usefully applied, to the admiration of the present age, will be the object of praise and commendation to those who come after us.** But this is to be done without interfering with sacred studies, as Our same Predecessor described in these most weighty words: *If you carefully search for the cause of those errors you will find that it lies in the fact that in these days when the natural sciences absorb so much study, the more severe and lofty studies have been proportionately neglected—some of them have almost passed into oblivion, some of them are pursued in a half-hearted or superficial way, and, sad to say, now that the splendour of the former estate is dimmed, they have been disfigured by perverse doctrines and monstrous errors,*† We ordain, therefore, that the study of natural sciences in the seminaries be carried out according to the law.

[2.—PRACTICAL APPLICATION]

2. All these prescriptions, both Our own and those of Our Predecessor, are to be kept in view whenever

* Leo XIII., Alloc., March 7, 1880.

† Loco. cit.

there is question of choosing directors and professors for seminaries and Catholic Universities. Anyone who in any way is found to be tainted with Modernism is to be excluded without compunction from these offices, whether of government or of teaching, and those who already occupy them are to be removed. The same policy is to be adopted towards those who openly or secretly lend countenance to Modernism either by extolling the Modernists and excusing their culpable conduct, or by carping at scholasticism, and the Fathers, and the magisterium of the Church, or by refusing obedience to ecclesiastical authority in any of its depositaries; and towards those who show a love of novelty in history, archæology, biblical exegesis; and finally towards those who neglect the sacred sciences or appear to prefer to them the secular. In all this question of studies, Venerable Brethren, you cannot be too watchful or too constant, but most of all in the choice of professors, for as a rule the students are modelled after the pattern of their masters. Strong in the consciousness of your duty, act always in this matter with prudence and with vigour.

Equal diligence and severity are to be used in examining and selecting candidates for Holy Orders. Far, far from the clergy be the love of novelty! God hateth the proud and the obstinate mind. For the future the doctorate of theology and canon law must never be conferred on anyone who has not first of all made the regular course of scholastic philosophy; if conferred, it shall be held as null and void. The rules laid down in 1896 by the Sacred Congregation of Bishops and Regulars for the clerics, both secular and regular, of Italy, concerning the frequenting of the Universities, We now decree to be extended to all nations. Clerics and priests inscribed in a Catholic Institute or University must not in the future follow in civil Universities those courses for which there are chairs in the Catholic Institutes to which they belong. If this has been permitted anywhere in the past, We ordain that it be not allowed for the future. Let the Bishops who form the Governing Board of such Catholic Institutes or Universities watch with all care that these Our commands be constantly observed.

[3.—EPISCOPAL VIGILANCE OVER PUBLICATIONS]

3. It is also the duty of the Bishops to prevent writings of Modernists, or whatever savours of Modernism or promotes it, from being read when they have been published, and to hinder their publication when they have not. No books or papers or periodicals whatever of this kind are to be permitted to seminarists or university students. The injury to them would be not less than that which is caused by immoral reading—nay, it would be greater, for

such writings poison Christian life at its very fount. The same decision is to be taken concerning the writings of some Catholics, who, though not evilly disposed themselves, are ill-instructed in theological studies and imbued with modern philosophy, and strive to make this harmonise with the faith, and, as they say, to turn it to the profit of the faith. The name and reputation of these authors cause them to be read without suspicion, and they are, therefore, all the more dangerous in gradually preparing the way for Modernism.

To add some more general directions, Venerable Brethren, in a matter of such moment, We order that you do everything in your power to drive out of your dioceses, even by solemn interdict, any pernicious books that may be in circulation there. The Holy See neglects no means to remove writings of this kind, but their number has now grown to such an extent that it is hardly possible to subject them all to censure. Hence it happens sometimes that the remedy arrives too late, for the disease has taken root during the delay. We will, therefore, that the Bishops, putting aside all fear and the prudence of the flesh, despising the clamour of evil men, shall, gently, by all means, but firmly, do each his own part in this work, remembering the injunctions of Leo XIII. in the Apostolic Constitution *Officiorum : Let the Ordinaries, acting in this also as Delegates of the Apostolic See, exert themselves to proscribe and to put out of reach of the faithful injurious books or other writings printed or circulated in their dioceses.* In this passage the Bishops, it is true, receive an authorisation, but they have also a charge laid upon them. Let no Bishop think that he fulfils this duty by denouncing to us one or two books, while a great many others of the same kind are being published and circulated. Nor are you to be deterred by the fact that a book has obtained elsewhere the permission which is commonly called the *Imprimatur*, both because this may be merely simulated, and because it may have been granted through carelessness or too much indulgence or excessive trust placed in the author, which last has perhaps sometimes happened in the religious orders. Besides, just as the same food does not agree with everyone, it may happen that a book, harmless in one place, may, on account of the different circumstances, be hurtful in another. Should a Bishop, therefore, after having taken the advice of prudent persons, deem it right to condemn any such books in his diocese, We give him ample faculty for the purpose and We lay upon him the obligation of doing so. Let all this be done in a fitting manner, and in certain cases it will suffice to restrict the prohibition to the clergy; but in all cases it will be obligatory on Catholic booksellers not to put on sale books condemned by the Bishop. And while We are treating of this subject, We wish the Bishops to see to it that booksellers do not, through desire for gain, engage in evil trade. It is certain that in the catalogues of some of them the books of the Modernists are not unfrequently announced with no small praise. If they refuse obedience, let the Bishops, after due admonition, have no hesitation in depriving them of the title of Catholic booksellers. This applies, and with still more reason, to those who have the title of Episcopal booksellers. If they have that of Pontifical booksellers let them be denounced to the Apostolic See. Finally, We remind all of Article XXVI. of the above-mentioned Constitution *Officiorum: All those who have obtained an apostolic faculty to read and keep forbidden books, are not thereby authorised to read and keep books and periodicals forbidden by the local Ordinaries unless the apostolic faculty expressly concedes permission to read and keep books condemned by any one whomsoever.*

### [4.—CENSORSHIP]

4. It is not enough to hinder the reading and the sale of bad books—it is also necessary to prevent them from being published. Hence, let the Bishops use the utmost strictness in granting permission to

print. Under the rules of the Constitution *Officiorum*, many publications require the authorisation of the Ordinary, and in certain dioceses (since the Bishop cannot personally make himself acquainted with them all) it has been the custom to have a suitable number of official censors for the examination of writings. We have the highest esteem for this institution of censors, and We not only exhort but We order that it be extended to all dioceses. In all episcopal Curias, therefore, let censors be appointed for the revision of works intended for publication, and let the censors be chosen from both ranks of the clergy—secular and regular—men whose age, knowledge, and prudence will enable them to follow the safe and golden mean in their judgments. It shall be their office to examine everything which requires permission for publication according to Articles XLI. and XLII. of the above-mentioned Constitution. The censor shall give his verdict in writing. If it be favourable, the Bishop will give the permission for publication by the word *Imprimatur*, which must be preceded by the *Nihil obstat* and the name of the censor. In the Roman Curia official censors shall be appointed in the same way as elsewhere, and the duty of nominating them shall appertain to the Master of the Sacred Palace, after they have been proposed to the Cardinal Vicar and have been approved and accepted by the Sovereign

Pontiff. It will also be the office of the Master of the Sacred Palace to select the censor for each writing. Permission for publication will be granted by him as well as by the Cardinal Vicar or his Vicegerent, and this permission, as above prescribed, must be preceded by the *Nihil obstat* and the name of the Censor. Only on very rare and exceptional occasions, and on the prudent decision of the Bishop, shall it be possible to omit mention of the Censor. The name of the Censor shall never be made known to the authors until he shall have given a favourable decision, so that he may not have to suffer inconvenience either while he is engaged in the examination of a writing or in case he should withhold his approval. Censors shall never be chosen from the religious orders until the opinion of the Provincial, or in Rome, of the General, has been privately obtained, and the Provincial or the General must give a conscientious account of the character, knowledge, and orthodoxy of the candidate. We admonish religious superiors of their most solemn duty never to allow anything to be published by any of their subjects without permission from themselves and from the Ordinary. Finally, We affirm and declare that the title of Censor with which a person may be honoured has no value whatever, and can never be adduced to give credit to the private opinions of him who holds it.

[PRIESTS AS EDITORS]

Having said this much in general, We now ordain in particular a more careful observance of Article XLII. of the above-mentioned Constitution *Officiorum*, according to which *it is forbidden to secular priests, without the previous consent of the Ordinary, to undertake the editorship of papers or periodicals.* This permission shall be withdrawn from any priest who makes a wrong use of it after having received an admonition thereupon. With regard to priests who are *correspondents* or *collaborators* of periodicals, as it happens not unfrequently that they contribute matter infected with Modernism to their papers or periodicals, let the Bishops see to it that they do not offend in this manner; and if they do, let them warn the offenders and prevent them from writing. We solemnly charge in like manner the superiors of religious orders that they fulfil the same duty, and should they fail in it, let the Bishops make due provision with authority from the Supreme Pontiff. Let there be, as far as this is possible, a special Censor for newspapers and periodicals written by Catholics. It shall be his office to read in due time each number after it has been published, and if he find anything dangerous in it let him order that it be corrected as soon as possible. The Bishop shall have the same right even when the Censor has seen nothing objectionable in a publication.

[5.—CONGRESSES]

5. We have already mentioned congresses and public gatherings as among the means used by the Modernists to propagate and defend their opinions. In the future, Bishops shall not permit Congresses of priests except on very rare occasions. When they do permit them it shall only be on condition that matters appertaining to the Bishops or the Apostolic See be not treated in them, and that no resolutions or petitions be allowed that would imply a usurpation of sacred authority, and that absolutely nothing be said in them which savours of Modernism, Presbyterianism, or Laicism. At Congresses of this kind, which can only be held after permission in writing has been obtained in due time and for each case, it shall not be lawful for priests of other dioceses to be present without the written permission of their Ordinary. Further, no priest must lose sight of the solemn recommendation of Leo XIII.: *Let priests hold as sacred the authority of their pastors, let them take it for certain that the sacerdotal ministry, if not exercised under the guidance of the Bishops, can never be either holy, nor very fruitful, nor worthy of respect.**

---

* Lett. Encyc. *Nobilissima Gallorum*, 10 Feb., 1884.

[6.—DIOCESAN VIGILANCE COMMITTEES]

6. But of what avail, Venerable Brethren, would be all Our commands and prescriptions if they be not dutifully and firmly carried out? In order that this may be done it has seemed expedient to us to extend to all dioceses the regulations which the Bishops of Umbria, with great wisdom, laid down for theirs many years ago.

"*In order,*" they say, "*to extirpate the errors already propagated and to prevent their further diffusion, and to remove those teachers of impiety through whom the pernicious effects of such diffusion are being perpetuated, this sacred Assembly, following the example of S. Charles Borromeo, has decided to establish in each of the dioceses a Council consisting of approved members of both branches of the clergy, which shall be charged with the task of noting the existence of errors and the devices by which new ones are introduced and propagated, and to inform the Bishop of the whole, so that he may take counsel with them as to the best means for suppressing the evil at the outset and preventing it spreading for the ruin of souls or, worse still, gaining strength and growth.*" * We decree, therefore, that in every diocese a council of this kind, which We are pleased to name the "Council of Vig-

* Acts of the Congress of the Bishops of Umbria, November, 1849, tit. 2, art. 6.

ilance," be instituted without delay. The priests called to form part in it shall be chosen somewhat after the manner above prescribed for the Censors, and they shall meet every two months on an appointed day in the presence of the Bishop. They shall be bound to secrecy as to their deliberations and decisions, and in their functions shall be included the following: They shall watch most carefully for every trace and sign of Modernism both in publications and in teaching, and to preserve it from the clergy and the young they shall take all prudent, prompt and efficacious measures. Let them combat novelties of words, remembering the admonitions of Leo XIII.: * *It is impossible to approve in Catholic publications a style inspired by unsound novelty which seems to deride the piety of the faithful and dwells on the introduction of a new order of Christian life, on new directions of the Church, on new aspirations of the modern soul, on a new social vocation of the clergy, on a new Christian civilisation, and many other things of the same kind.*

Language of the kind here indicated is not to be tolerated either in books or in lectures. The Councils must not neglect the books treating of the pious traditions of different places or of sacred relics. Let them not permit such questions to be discussed in journals or periodicals destined to foster piety,

* Instruct. S.C. NN. EE. EE., January 27, 1902.

neither with expressions savouring of mockery or contempt, nor by dogmatic pronouncements, especially when, as is often the case, what is stated as a certainty either does not pass the limits of probability or is based on prejudiced opinion. Concerning sacred relics, let this be the rule: if Bishops, who alone are judges in such matters, know for certain that a relic is not genuine, let them remove it at once from the veneration of the faithful; if the authentications of a relic happen to have been lost through civil disturbances, or in any other way, let it not be exposed for public veneration until the Bishop has verified it. The argument of prescription or well-founded presumption is to have weight only when devotion to a relic is commendable by reason of its antiquity, according to the sense of the Decree issued in 1896 by the Congregation of Indulgences and Sacred Relics: *Ancient relics are to retain the veneration they have always enjoyed except when in individual instances there are clear arguments that they are false or supposititious.* In passing judgment on pious traditions let it always be borne in mind that in this matter the Church uses the greatest prudence, and that she does not allow traditions of this kind to be narrated in books except with the utmost caution and with the insertion of the declaration imposed by Urban VIII.; and even then she does not guarantee the truth of the fact narrated;

she simply does not forbid belief in things for which human evidence is not wanting. On this matter the Sacred Congregation of Rites, thirty years ago, decreed as follows: *These apparitions or revelations have neither been approved nor condemned by the Holy See, which has simply allowed them to be believed on purely human faith, on the tradition which they relate, corroborated by testimony and documents worthy of credence.* * Any one who follows this rule has no cause to fear. For the devotion based on any apparition, in so far as it regards the fact itself, that is to say, in as far as the devotion is *relative*, always implies the condition of the fact being true; while in as far as it is *absolute*, it is always based on the truth, seeing that its object is the persons of the saints who are honoured. The same is true of relics. Finally, We entrust to the Councils of Vigilance the duty of overlooking assiduously and diligently social institutions as well as writings on social questions so that they may harbour no trace of Modernism, but obey the prescriptions of the Roman Pontiffs.

### [7.—TRIENNIAL RETURNS]

7. Lest what We have laid down thus far should pass into oblivion, We will and ordain that the Bishops of all dioceses, a year after the publication of these letters and every three years thenceforward,

* Decree, May 2, 1877.

furnish the Holy See with a diligent and sworn report on the things which have been decreed in this Our Letter, and on the doctrines that find currency among the clergy, and especially in the seminaries and other Catholic institutions, those not excepted which are not subject to the Ordinary, and We impose the like obligation on the Generals of Religious Orders with regard to those who are under them.

[CONCLUSION]

This, Venerable Brethren, is what We have thought it Our duty to write to you for the salvation of all who believe. The adversaries of the Church will doubtlessly abuse what We have said to refurbish the old calumny by which We are traduced as the enemy of science and of the progress of humanity. As a fresh answer to such accusations, which the history of the Christian religion refutes by never-failing evidence, it is Our intention to establish by every means in our power a special Institute in which, through the co-operation of those Catholics who are most eminent for their learning, the advance of science and every other department of knowledge may be promoted under the guidance and teaching of Catholic truth. God grant that We may happily realise Our design with the assistance of all those who bear a sincere love for the Church of Christ. But of this We propose to speak on another occasion.

Meanwhile, Venerable Brethren, fully confident in your zeal and energy, We beseech for you with Our whole heart the abundance of heavenly light, so that in the midst of this great danger to souls from the insidious invasions of error upon every hand, you may see clearly what ought to be done, and labour to do it with all your strength and courage. May Jesus Christ, the author and finisher of our faith, be with you in His power; and may the Immaculate Virgin, the destroyer of all heresies, be with you by her prayers and aid. And We, as a pledge of Our affection and of the Divine solace in adversity, most lovingly grant to you, your clergy and people, the Apostolic Benediction.

*Given at S. Peter's, Rome, on the eighth day of September, one thousand nine hundred and seven, the fifth year of our Pontificate.*

PIUS X., POPE.

THE END